SHADOWS
ON THE
MOUNTAIN

POEMS AND LYRICS
1976–1989

BY
C. COOPER ARD

"Shadows On The Mountain," by C. Cooper Ard. ISBN 978-1-60264-405-2 (Softcover); ISBN 978-1-60264-406-9 (Hardcover).

Published 2009 by Virtualbookworm.com Publishing Inc., P.O. Box 9949, College Station, TX 77842, US. ©2009, C. Cooper Ard. All rights reserved. No part of this publication may be reproduced, stored in a retrieval system, or transmitted in any form or by any means, electronic, mechanical, recording or otherwise, without the prior written permission of C. Cooper Ard.

Manufactured in the United States of America.

THIS BOOK IS DEDICATED TO

Paul, Stan, Mike, Bela, Joe, Steve, George, Lon, Mark,
John, Mike, Richie, Jack, Pierre, John, Boris, Norrin,
Mike, Jim, Roy, Mrs. Lewis, Mark, Lee, Scott, Glyn,
Layne, David, John, Lou, Tom, Joey, Kerry,
Tami & Ty, Paul, James, Charles, Steve,
and all the loves left behind...

SHADOWS ON THE MOUNTAIN

All my life I've been on the road
It never seemed strange to me
Move away every couple of years
There's more places to be

Meeting new people nearly every day
Seemed like the thing to do
Now the time has come to see what I've done
And look at what I've been through

Shadows on the mountain
Saucers in the sky
I haven't seen everything
Just enough to get me by

Now I may be going crazy
Or I may be going straight
But I think I know from the places I go
We all have a change of state

I've got no place to call my home
No place to settle down
Not Bossier, Bellevue or Wichita Falls
I just can't find my town!

I've been from Minot to Warner Robins
But I can't look to the past
I've got to find a new place
And I've got to make it last

Shadows on the mountain
Saucers in the sky
I haven't seen everything
Just enough to get me by

Now I may be going crazy
Or I may be going straight
But I think I know from the places I go
We all have a change of state

4

Now I'm right on the breadth of a dream
I'm beginning to see the light
I've been making the social scene
And I think I've been doing it right

Living out of a suitcase
Is really not my way
But I won't let that bother me
I'm heading for that "Big A"!

Shadows on the mountain
Saucers in the sky
I haven't seen everything
Just enough to get me by

Now I may be going crazy
Or I may be going straight
But I think I know from the places I go
We all have a change of state

Brighten up those shadows
Climb the highest peak
Haven't seen no U.F.O.
But that's not all I seek

A house, a car and money
Are some of the things I'd like
But without some love to back them up
Then I'd rather be riding a bike!

Wo! Shadows on the mountain
Saucers in the sky
I haven't seen everything
Just enough to get me by

Now I may be going crazy
Or I may be going straight
But I think I know from the places I go
That I don't want to get there late.

1978

CONTENTS

CLOUDS OF CONFUSION

NOW HERE COME
THE FULL MOON!

INTRODUCTION

Why now? Why publish a book of poetry a full score after the last piece was actually written? Well, the idea of collecting these scattered poems and song lyrics has been on my mind for over a decade now. However, sometimes life gets in the way of even the most determined inspiration. So after months of digging and compiling, you are now holding in your hands the completed work.

When I say completed, that is pretty much the case here. This volume contains the full breadth of my poetic output. The good and the bad, the happy and the sad; as they say. It's guaranteed that you, the reader, will not find every poem included here a great piece of art. The variety of topics and subject matter is so wide they could not all possibly appeal to any one person. My hope is that at least somewhere among these hundred or so pieces, you will find something that makes you smile, be thoughtful, relate, reflect, laugh or stir your emotions in some way.

I hesitate when I say, "my poetic output." You see, I've always had a hard time claiming credit for my poems. It's difficult to explain, but I've often felt that they really just wrote themselves. Dozens of times, I would not be able to sleep at night because a lyric or whole verses would mysteriously appear in my head. Inevitably, I would have to get up and write them down on paper just to get it out of my system. Other times, I may have just been driving in my car and suddenly a tune would come to me and I would instantly start singing it. By the time I reached my destination, the song would be complete. If only all of life were so easy.

For a decade and a half, it's as if I was a vessel for some kind of poetic machine and my task was to capture the words and rhymes on paper. To put black on white. Often times, I would be a workmanlike craftsman as well. I could sit down with only a title or maybe a single line and within an hour or so, bang out a complete poem. Again, once I got started, the words and amazingly appropriate rhymes would magically form in my mind. It was my job just to get the structure right and decide on the sequence of the verses, bridges and choruses.

For this book, my initial thought was to have everything appear chronologically. Just lay it all out there as it happened from beginning to end. However, I was persuaded by a friend to group the poems thematically. Therefore, the book is divided into ten chapters so that as you're reading each piece within a chapter, it should share some commonality to the others around it. At the end of each one, I included the year it was first written so that you can still get a perspective of the order in which they were composed.

Those of you familiar with the Ladders and Moondogs may notice some differences from the recorded lyrics and the versions that appear in this book. While I was going through my files and putting together this collection, I came across numerous versions of the lyrics. Most of them hand-written on standard notebook paper, but many on odd size scrap paper, backs of envelopes, napkins or anything I could find at the moment when the words originally came to me.

I started to put the different versions of each piece together. As I read through them one by one, I noticed verses here and there that were omitted from the final recorded versions. Most often this was due to time constraints of the particular song we were working on. Reading these missing lyrics again for the first time in decades was like discovering old friends. They were familiar to me, but had not been engrained in my brain like the recorded songs have.

So exercising my poetic license, I decided to see if I could work them back in. I had to move a few things around here and there and even come up with a few new lines to finish out some incomplete verses. What we have now is the equivalent of bonus material or extended versions of many of the pieces. It was fun working with all the poems and lyrics again and I have been well-pleased with the results. I hope you will too.

LOVES LEFT BEHIND

It's Hard
For the Love of Death
Valentine Card
Stronger Than a Sunrise
Tear of Joy
Your Door
Ain't Nuthin' (Bigger Than a Dinosaur)
Can I See You Tomorrow?
Love Expense
Fascination
Lonesome Lover
When the Night Falls
Tell You
You Love Me
Long Distance Lover
People in Love
Thoughts
When You Were Here
White Pearl
Pieces of a Puzzle
Face in the Moon
Sometimes
Love is Gone

IT'S HARD

A love I left behind has since followed me
To the ends of the world for my eyes to see

A life that I've forgotten has called for my return
I know that I should leave so that I may learn
The way to take me back is not to miss my turn

But it's so hard
Yes, it's hard
My love I'll guard
You know it's hard

Reflections of the past are cast upon the lake
Where moonlight mends our minds till morning we shall wake
To see the sun that shines upon the love we make

It's hard to understand the workings of my mind
It's hard to be a man and still treat you kind
It's hard to think of you as anyone else would
It's hard to love you true as I know I could

Although it's hard to try
I would rather die than to see you cry over losing me
Can't you see?

Now hand in hand and cheek to cheek
I know you can and I hear you speak:
Stay with me more than ever
That our love may last forever.

1977

FOR THE LOVE OF DEATH

The touch of Death came late last night
He took her from my arms
She left without a single cry
He lured her with his charms

In peace she died upon the bed
In silence and with style
And though she died most painfully
Her face, it wore a smile

This love of mine was good and kind
Of harm she could not bring
Her skin was soft and thus would glow
Like flowers in the spring

Her lips were full as moon is bright
Her eyes, a shining green
Her hair was dark like sky at night
As dark as I have seen

I met my love some time ago
While shopping in a store
Although she was to marry me
There was something she loved more

While driving home one rainy night
A graveyard we did see
Her eyes were locked upon the dead
A chill came over me

For the love of death
For the love of death
For the love of death, I cry
For the love of death
She lost her breath
For the love of death, goodbye

I called to her as I came in
It was toward the end of day
There was no answer; she was gone
My mind it seemed to say:

"Where could she be this cloudy day?
Oh please, oh please not there!"
The graveyard whispered cold and bleak
Her hands were raised in prayer

I pulled her from the musty tomb
And not a word was said
Until at home she spoke with joy
"To live is to be dead!"

She called the Reaper from below
To claim her when she died
His charm of death had brought an end
To my beloved bride

I'm sure my love is happy now
Beneath the earthen ground
I call on Death to claim me now
To see what she has found

For the love of death
For the love of death
For the love of death, I cry
For the love of death
She lost her breath
For the love of death, goodbye.

1977

VALENTINE CARD

Love and Spring
The two are one
The birds will sing
To everyone

Smiles will glow
And sun will rise
Flowers grow
Before our eyes

Green are the trees
Soft is the ground
Love is the breeze
That blows us around

Time is a wheel
From end to start
The love I feel
Is from my heart

I give to you
This Valentine
My love is true
You must be mine.

1977

STRONGER THAN A SUNRISE

I get up every morning to the same old day
Listen to me world, I got something to say
Sometimes you're good to me, sometimes you're bad
But now you took away what I never had
Oh yeah, oh yeah – what I never had

And now every time it's dawn, reminds me that my girl is gone
She left me real early that day
Now she's oh so far away and all the people say:

"We told you so
You know that we told you so
That girl just had to go
You know we told you so
You know that we told you so"

But I tend to disagree
You just didn't see
That look in her eyes
It was stronger than a sunrise

And I said, "Baby, you're stronger than a sunrise
I can see it in your eyes
Please don't leave me now
I'll make it up somehow"

That's when she turned her head
She tried a smile and then she said,
"Honey, you're stronger than a sunrise
I can see it in your eyes
You just go on without me then we'll both be living free"

'Cause we're both stronger than a sunrise
We can see it in our eyes
We're both too strong to live together
Maybe now it'll work out better.

1977

TEAR OF JOY

Once I had loved you and in fact, I still do
But then, nothing happened and I've no one to blame but you
We worked so close together; never far apart
You never gave me your love, but I gave you my heart

I kept hanging around you, but you kept letting me down
You sure knew how to stall 'cause you never answered my call
You left me here all alone
Now I'm chilled to the bone
You never answered my call...

Hey, hey, hey – what do ya say?
I learned to play that game today
You moved to the left – I moved to the right
Can I take you home tonight?

Hey, I wanna be loved by you
Yes, I do – you know it's true
Say, do you wanna be loved by me?
Can't you see that I want to be with you?

You left a tear of joy with your song of happiness
Your song of happiness has filled my heart
Now you've made me see that you are here for me
And I am here for you – may we never break apart

We've seen that show so many times that it has filled our minds
With never needed information; turn it into inspiration

Won't you come with me so you can always be
In a place that we can share?
They say we make such a perfect pair

You have that shining smile that always drives me wild
And though it's been so many years
You are always in my eyes and ears.

1978

22

YOUR DOOR

Your door
I've been standing at your door
Just like I've done before
I can't ask you anymore

I have been so all alone
That many times I've wept
I have seen the face I've known
Even while I've slept

So won't you please
Please answer me
Come to your door...

You've closed me out of your life
Is it because of other men?
Only you can be my wife
So open your door and let me in

I wish that I could stay
Remember those days on the windy plains?
Has it all been washed away
Like the snow and the rains?

Now I lie awake at night
With the heart you tore
It isn't right so please answer...

Your door
I've been waiting at your door
Just like I've done before (don't keep me waiting)
I won't ask you anymore
Come to your door

So many tears
So many tears.

1980

AIN'T NUTHIN' (BIGGER THAN A DINOSAUR)

There's no stopping me now
Now that I've come to know
Know what you're all about
I tell you, baby I know

I keep calling you up
Up into the stars if I have to
Girl, you better see me
'Cause I just gotta see you

Ain't nuthin' bigger than a dinosaur
Ain't nuthin' longer than a mile or two
Ain't nuthin' faster than a silver board
Ain't nuthin' stronger than my love for you

So many times I have waited so long
For the right love
The love that never came along

So give it all to me
I want more than just a part
A part is all right, but I want you to fill my heart

Ain't nuthin' bigger than a dinosaur
Ain't nuthin' longer than a mile or two
Ain't nuthin' faster than a silver board
Ain't nuthin' stronger than my love for you

I'm still calling you up
Up into the stars every night
Girl, I'm looking at you
And there ain't a more beautiful sight

Ain't nuthin'
Ain't nuthin'
Ain't nuthin' bigger than a dinosaur.

1981

CAN I SEE YOU TOMORROW?

Can I see you tomorrow?
Oh baby, won't you please say "yes"
Can I see you tomorrow?
You've really got my mind in a mess
Can I see you tomorrow?
Oh baby, you're truly the best
Can I see you tomorrow?
You know I love you more than the rest

And now I must get to you somehow before my heart aches out
You see it's time we both agree to let our love break out
We've got to go; we've got to show our feelings too
I want to give; I want to live my life with you

Can I see you tomorrow?
My love keeps getting stronger
Can I see you tomorrow?
I just can't wait any longer
Can I see you tomorrow?
I'd rather see you tonight
Can I see you tomorrow?
I'll meet you down by the light

Can I love you forever?
That's all I want to do
I need you more than ever
I hope you need me too
Can I see you tomorrow?
Don't let anything stand in your way
Can I see you tomorrow?
It's going to be a beautiful day

(Can he see you tomorrow?)
Oh baby, please end my sorrow
(Can he see you tomorrow?)
Oh baby, how much time can I borrow?

1981

LOVE EXPENSE

Pretend she doesn't exist
Pretend you never knew her
I think I'm falling out of love
It's time you out grew her
This time you'd better forget her
Don't let her break your heart
You know it's happened before
It really tore you apart

Love expense; love expense
You paid for it all and it makes no sense
Love expense; love expense
Just write it off as a love expense

So why don't you stop fooling yourself
And move in a new direction?
By keeping her off of your mind
You'll make the correction
But you say, "She was special"
Well, that don't mean anything
Because she doesn't really love you
You're only playing second string

Love expense; love expense
You paid for it all and it makes no sense
Love expense; love expense
Just write it off as a love expense

So you cleared her account, but you gave it one last look
The figures didn't balance and that's not all she took!

Love expense; love expense
You paid for it all and it makes no sense
Love expense; love expense
Just write it off as a love expense
Just write it off as a love expense.

1981

FASCINATION

You have this hold over me and I can't let it be
Impossible to look away
'Cause there's something about you that makes me feel so true
This is what I have to say:

I'm using concentration as well as my imagination
To try to figure you out
You've got determination and you're my inspiration
This is what it's all about...

Fascination, fascination, fascination
I've got this fascination with you...

We're dancing in my dreams; we're so close together
Everything is what it seems; we're as light as a feather
I look into your eyes searching for a sign
After so many tries I've made you mine

You have this hold over me and I can't let it be
Impossible to turn away
'Cause there's something about you that makes me feel so true
This is what I have to say:

I'm using concentration as well as my imagination
To try to figure you out
You've got determination and you're my inspiration
This is what it's all about...

Fascination, fascination, fascination
I've got this fascination with you...

We're dancing in my dreams; we're so happy together
Everything is what it seems; we're as light as a feather
I stare into your eyes searching for a sign
After so many tries I've made you mine.

1981

LONESOME LOVER

Her heart's on fire
She's wound up inside
Late at night she's even cried
She's gone to church to pray for him
But his chances are looking very slim
He doesn't seem to care about Heaven or Hell
He likes it here and he's doing well
Sometimes she thinks she'll never get through
Love frustration is nothing new
She lives her life always wearing a smile
Maybe he'll come out in a little while

Lonesome lover
Lonesome lover
You can't get him out of your mind

Lonesome lover
You must discover how not to get left behind

Her heart leaps up when he comes home
She stays close and she'll never roam
So she stands there and stares at him
With one eye up, he looks so grim
Then she turns her head and begins to sigh
She must hold back that tear in her eye
He says a few words then walks away
She just can't seem to make him stay
He slips inside as her girlfriend calls
They'll walk around when the night falls

Lonesome lover
He's undercover
Hiding behind his wall

Lonesome lover
You must recover from this lonely fall.

1981

WHEN THE NIGHT FALLS

When the night falls
The cat calls and the wind starts to blow
The lovers wait; they hesitate
They don't really know
They're afraid they'll miss the final kiss
Before they have to go in
The lovers wait; it's too late
What will happen to them?

When the night falls upon the children of the neighborhood
They walk around and around and around
The darkness makes them feel so good
And music fills the air until a thunderstorm blows it all away
When the night falls it brings the end to still another day

When the night falls
The car stalls, but nobody opens the door
It's not too late; it's just a date
Or could it be something more?
When love is the key we all agree
We make it to give
Unlock the heart; the place to start
That's where we all live

When the night falls upon the children of the neighborhood
They walk around and around and around
The darkness makes them feel so good
And music fills the air until a thunderstorm blows it all away
When the night falls it brings the end to still another day

When the night falls, her Mom calls and the wind starts to blow
The lovers wait; they hesitate
They don't really know
But they won't miss their only kiss even in the pouring rain
The lovers wait; it feels great – no need to explain
When the night falls.

1981

TELL YOU

All of you don't understand
Just what it is to be a lonely man
You've got each other to be with
A couple of drinks; maybe a fourth or fifth
But now I've got something to say
It's going to be different today

(How's that?)

Yes, I'm going to tell you, tell you, tell you
Tell you about my girl
Tell you about my friend
Tell you about my girlfriend
And how we've been getting along
Singing our song
Doing what's right and never what's wrong

Yes, I'm going to tell you, tell you, tell you
Tell you all about her now
Tell you about my love
Tell you about all that and the things I've been thinking of

(Ah—but we saw you walking there
Why you even combed your hair)

Yes, I looked nice and I paid the full price

(Ah—but was that really you?
You must be honest and true)

Yes, that was me and I'll make you see

Because I'm going to tell you, tell you, tell you
Tell you all about her now
Tell you about my love
Tell you about all that and the things I've been thinking of.

1981

30

YOU LOVE ME

You say that you love me but you don't understand
Am I just a little boy or am I a man?
Well, who am I now?
I don't really know
So please won't you help me to make my love show

Baby, you're just too young
Maybe I'm just too old
Your heart burns too hot while mine is too cold

You say that you love me
So what will we do?
I'm still hiding secrets that I just can't tell you

You loved me then; you love me now
Why can't I ever say it somehow?
You love me today; you love me tonight
Why can't I ever say it just right?

I think that I want you because I need love too
I look in your brown eyes but I'm still seeing blue
Are you just too young?
Perhaps I'm just too old
You see, your love burns too hot while I'm just too cold

So who am I now?
I really don't know
So please won't you help me so our love can flow

You love me shy; you love me wild
Yet deep inside I'm still a child
You love me more; you love me a lot
Yet so far you're all I've got

But I'll try my best to make you see
And I'll hand you my heart when you say you love me.

1981

LONG DISTANCE LOVER

Hello, how ya doin'?
Are you feeling all right?
Hello, how ya doin'?
Can we talk tonight?

I've been sitting here waiting by my telephone
Just hoping to hear you 'cause I'm all alone

Long distance lover don't go undercover
I'll never find another; we're so far apart
Long distance lover; you're unlike any other
I'm trying to discover the way to your heart

Talk, talk on the telephone
Talk, talk; have to make it known
Talk, talk; aren't we all alone sometimes?

I've fallen in love though we've never met
I know it sounds crazy but my mind is set
You're a special someone and I'm willing to bet
That you're like no other

You're more than just a voice on the other end
I write about you in the letters I send
Somehow I feel that you're more than a friend
My long distance lover

Talk, talk on the telephone
Talk, talk; have to make it known
Talk, talk; aren't we all alone sometimes?

Somewhere out there is a heart with a beat
For another in the world to make it complete
Many hearts beat away before they can meet
Their long distance lovers

But me, I'm a very fortunate man
You found me, woman, in the heart of a band
Peace, love and happiness is all we understand
My long distance lover

Talk, talk on the telephone
Talk, talk; have to make it known
Talk, talk; aren't we all alone sometimes?

Talk, talk on the telephone
Dial direct when you're at home
Talk, talk; aren't we all alone somehow?

Talk, talk, talk to me tonight
Talk, talk; are you feeling all right?
Talk, talk; wish I could hold you tight right now

Goodbye, call you later
My long distance lover
Goodbye, catch you later
They'll never be another, it's true
Goodnight babe, I love you.

1982

PEOPLE IN LOVE

I said, "Hey...what'cha doing in love?"
Wouldn't you know I'm all alone
I said, "Say...you people in love
Tell me what I need to know"

I said, "Hey...what'cha doing in love?
Can't you see I'm all alone?"
I said, "Say...you people in love
Tell me what I need to know
Before you go, before you go, before you go"

Leave out the heartaches; leave out the pain
Leave out the sorrows; tears in the rain
Leave out the bad times; don't want to fight
Leave out your troubles; cries in the night

People in love have a lot to live for
People in love don't need any more

I said, "Hey...you people in love
Can't you tell I want some too?"
I said, "Say...you people in love
Tell me what I need to do"

Take her out to dinner; take her for a ride
Take her to a movie; hold her by my side
Show her a good time; oh, what a sight!
Take her home later; kiss her goodnight

People in love got their feet in the door
People in love have a lot to live for.

1982

THOUGHTS

Thoughts of me – thoughts of you
Thoughts of things we used to do... together
Thoughts of you – thoughts of me
Thoughts of who we used to be... together

Memories of the moonlight upon the window panes
Reminds me of that June night and the summer rains
Thunderstorms time and again
A part of every day
Until finally my friend
They washed you away

Thinking of your thoughtfulness
Thinking of your smiles
Thinking of your tenderness
Forever in my files
Recalling your reflections
Studying my styles
Thinking of you all alone
Across so many miles

Life ends in a cul-de-sac
An empty home tonight
I'm no longer keeping track
The mailbox is sealed tight

Remember recollections
Your visions of the past
Start planning new directions
The dreams will always last

Thoughts of me – thoughts of you
Thoughts of what we used to do... together

Remember you – remember me
Remember too we used to be... together.

1982

WHEN YOU WERE HERE

A decade of knowing year after year
A decade of growing when you were here

Because when you were here
We never felt alone
No matter where our house might be
You were always in our home

We could always make you smile
When we scratched behind your ears
Now all those happy moments
Have given way to tears

You always seemed so satisfied
Then there was the time we tried
To hide away our fear
But number nine finally came
And it will never be the same
As it was when you were here

You were truly one of us
We loved you in a special way
We really miss your presence now
And wish you were here today

Thank you for the warmth you gave
You're welcome for the attention
We thank you for so many things
Too numerous to mention

A decade of living year after year
A decade of giving when you were here

1982

WHITE PEARL

White Pearl—Light Girl
Won't you tell me your name?
In my court, I play the sport
It's really not my game

Your skin is fair; I can only stare
At the eyes on your face
I look so deep when I'm asleep
You move with such grace

White Pearl—Light Girl
Won't you give me a chance?
White Pearl—Light Girl
I want you to dance

With the love of the world
You could build a tall mountain
And climb it all the way to the sky
With the love of this girl
I could build a small fortune
And spend it till the day I die

White Pearl—Light Girl
Won't you give me a chance?
White Pearl—Light Girl
I want you to dance, dance, dance!

White Pearl—Light Girl
Won't you tell me your name?
White Pearl—Light Girl
It's really all the same

White Pearl—Light Girl
Won't you give me a chance?
White Pearl—Light Girl
I want you to dance, dance, dance!.

1985

PIECES OF A PUZZLE

The pieces of a puzzle fall into place
Sometimes confusing but they fit their space
While we go together so perfectly fine
Though it hasn't been easy
I'm so glad you're mine

You're so understanding
You say what you feel
So drop all your doubts
Because this is for real

It's been so unfair
But you've withstood the pain
You've held back the hurt
From your eyes there's no rain

Separate and lonely is a life incomplete
To see the whole picture, the pieces must meet
We both must contribute as much as we can
To work on this puzzle as a woman and man

Complicated is the puzzle with the parts it's made of
The piecing together of two hearts in love
Emotional and physical in these ways we touch
I don't feel it's possible to love you too much

Though our desires are strong as we each have this need
The pieces are joining and our love will succeed.

1983

FACE IN THE MOON

I see your face in the moon and I wish I knew that tune
The one that you played me tonight
Yes, you knew it so well, but I knew that you could tell
That I would never play it right

So I sit here alone far away from my phone
Staring at your face in the sky
Oh, I'm looking for a clue so I'll know what to do
And I won't even ask you why

Because your face in the moon is worth more than a tune
And you mean more to me than just a song
Yes, your face is so bright that it lights up all the night
And I know that our love can't be wrong

Your face will look upon the stars while I drive among the cars
That cover this planet far below
Oh, how I long to see your face looking back at me
Tell me what it is I need to know

Face in the moon above me
Tell me that you love me
Tell me that you care
Tell me you'll be there

When you are so far away that I can't see you today
Please turn your face up towards the moon
Oh, of course I will do the same and I will call out your name
We will be together very soon

Because your face in the moon is worth more than a tune
And you mean more to me than just a song
Yes, your face is so bright that it lights up all the night
And I know that our love can't be wrong.

1983

SOMETIMES

Sometimes I will think of you
And I wonder just what to do
You broke my heart and I said goodbye
Did it really make you cry?

I was always so true to you
With each day my love only grew
But then you left me and went away
Your love had gone astray...

Sometimes I see that sparkle in your eyes
Now I realize that some love never dies

Miss you...(sometimes)
Need you...(sometimes)
Want you back now!

I'll take you back if you'll have me too
We'll do the things that we used to do
Deep in my heart, I still love you.

1984

LOVE IS GONE

...and now we must depart
Thrown away each other's heart
Given up on all the years
Drowning in a sea of tears
Promises in the dark
Picnics in Piedmont Park
Care free and cold ice cream
This was all a broken dream
I'm the one who said I could
You're the one who said you would
Went a while and then we stopped
You spoke to me, but I had dropped

Fell in love without thinking through
Not a wise thing to do
Hearts of manipulation created this situation
You're a window then a wall
First I write and then I call
Bridges of communication; walls of procrastination

Things went smooth; things went rough
You'd be sweet; I'd be tough
Cannot seem to get together
Emotions change like the weather
Hearts of joy while holding hands
Listening to a gear fab band
Pepper music in our ears
Helped us to forget our fears
Tunes with hauntful melodies
Always played in minor keys
Certain songs remain unsung
Love is never forever young
Wicked words have had their say
All dried up and blown away
And now our love is gone
Yet somehow we must go on...

1988

TO THE COSMOS

SOARING THROUGH THE UNIVERSE

SPACEMAN

SCORPIO

SOARING THROUGH THE UNIVERSE

From the beginning, I have known
As I've learned as well as grown
That the time has come at last
When I leave behind my past

My soul has left the rest of me
My spirit now, at last, is free
My mind has awaited this day
My being carries me away
Through cosmic right of birth
A blessing not a curse
I was meant to be
The guardian of the galaxy

I leave behind the shattered Earth
Soaring through the universe
Looking for a certain sign
That will show me what is mine
Flying lower or is it higher?
It matters not, it's my desire
Near Jupiter and Saturn after Mars
Through the darkness to the stars

Soaring through the endless void
Past meteors and asteroids
Leaving tracks others will trace
With shiny ships of golden grace
Soon to come are man's space stations
Among the heavens and constellations
Though called by some an astronaut
It is knowledge I have sought

To the cosmos, I am first
Soaring through the universe
Searching for that certain sign
That will show me what is mine.

1976

SPACEMAN

The Spaceman is a lonely man in his suit of white
Waiting in his capsule seat to blast off to the night
He'll be gone many months they say before he does return
He'll travel to a distant place where there is much to learn

He knows his job and he does it well
He's proud to be the one
He swears that he will not return before his task is done

He feels the rockets beneath him rise
The countdown is at end
Now he hears the voice of home
It is his only friend

Spaceman, silent Spaceman
Please tell us soon
The secret of the universe or just that of the moon

Spaceman, solo Spaceman
We're with you all the way
May your journey be a safe one to that place so far away

He gazes out his porthole at an asteroid
And thinks of what lies ahead in this endless void
The cosmos is so beautiful with suns of soaring heat
Other life must exist out there that he is sure to meet

He looks upon stars never seen by any Earthly man
And wonders, wishes and hopes that he will understand
He checks the panel one last time before he goes to sleep
All is silent in the craft except for one small beep

Spaceman, silent Spaceman
Oh, please tell us soon
The secret of the universe or just that of the moon

Spaceman, solo Spaceman
We're with you all the way
May your journey be a safe one to that place so far away

The Spaceman has arrived at last and walks now wide awake
Upon the sphere that he will study toward a steaming lake
It is just as he had thought; there is life here to be found
He grasps the plant-like structure and pulls it from the ground

Back to the ship he takes it with all that he has seen
Now he finally notices that his hand is turning green
He must never return to Earth and never hear them cheer
For the Spaceman who sits alone...
Down his green face rolls a tear

Spaceman, silent Spaceman
We have yet to hear from you
Have you made it to the sphere?
Have you discovered something new?

Spaceman, solo Spaceman
Please won't you heed our call?
Or is it true of what they say
That you don't care at all?

1977

SCORPIO

With the skyline of the trees and of the stars that float above the sky
Oh my, we have a windless night and a sky of velvet blue
Tell me, how are you
Scorpio?

Oh Scorpio
What do you really know?
You're always on the go
Scorpio

You say you feel the wind blow
Scorpio out my window
I really need you so
Scorpio

Oh Scorpio
I look from far below as you crawl across the sky
Oh my
You have one star of red that seems to make you glow
Scorpio

Oh Scorpio
What do you really know?
You're always on the go
Scorpio.

1978

HOME IS THE HERO

Home is the Hero

Prologue: Loneliness

Arrival and Departure

Come to Canada

Am I a Rain Man?

Arrival and Departure II

Like Fools in the Hills

Living in the Past

I'm Just a Sad Man

Am I a Rain Man? (Reprise)

Epilogue: Home is the Hero

HOME IS THE HERO

Home is the hero
He's come back at last
To the land of his friends
To the land of his past

He takes hold of their hands
And he looks in their eyes
As he falls to his knees
He lays down and cries

Home is the hero
Home is the hero

He's lived thru the years
But his time has expired
His loves are now gone
With all he desired

The sand has run out
The deadline draws near
He must make a choice
But the paths are unclear

Home is the hero
Home is the hero

His heart hangs now heavy
And he must say farewell
His voice must ring true
Like the ring of a bell

Yes, home is the hero
From out of the blue
"Who is he?" you ask
Well, he just could be you.

1977

PROLOGUE: LONELINESS

The wind blows not gentle
He blows in giant gusts
And I'm alone up here
Just me and my lusts

That's how it is and was
With no friends around
There's no sharing of thoughts
Or sights or sound

Just riding every day
And working out at night
What I'm trying to say is
It doesn't feel right

Writing letters where words would do
And when I send words, I want faces too

I know the pressure's off
I've had time to settle down
I'm king of my bedroom
So where's my royal crown?

But it's not all that bad
It's nice here in the day
I'm thinking hard, but just can't seem
To find any more to say

You see there's a story to be told
Not of love or epic battles
But of friends on vacation
In their car and in their saddles

While I was being lonely
Four were searching for a fifth
They found him here
And so it begins with...

1977

ARRIVAL AND DEPARTURE

...arrival of the four was really no surprise
It wasn't even 4:00 when they pulled in the drive

Preparations had been made earlier that day
Mattresses had been laid to comfort their stay

At first just smiles then some handshakes
They had come some miles to see the lakes

It was really great to talk with such good friends
It was more than fate that brought us to these ends

Together we ate dinner then out to play some jarts
Congratulate the winner though in our hearts
We knew that they had cheated, but "what the hell?"
We had been defeated, just said "Oh well"

Of course they stayed the night and even the next day
Keeping them was tight, but soon we'd go away

I showed them the base and drove them to town
There wasn't a trace of impression to be found

Back at this house of mine we packed up to go
I was feeling fine, but the trunk was getting low

We packed more than what we'd need, but we left anyway
And on that road northward
A voice just seemed to say...

1977

COME TO CANADA

Come to Canada
Where lakes are blue
Come to Canada
It's right for you

Come on up
Now hurry, honey
Come on up
And bring your money

You can drive on our roads at sixty miles per hour
Can't swim in the lakes so stick to the shower

When you reach the border where the Peace Gardens are
Stop for a look—get out of the car

We've got a great gift shop you'll find very nice
Get whatever you want—just pay the price

Come to Canada
Now hurry, honey
Come on up
And bring your money

Camping is cool if you find the right spot
Just drive around and pick out a lot

Deep in the woods, get yourselves lost
Camp where you'd like, but it's gonna cost

Just a reminder, check on the ground
In case you don't know, the ants are around

Come to Canada
Where lakes are blue
Come on up
It's right for you

From forests to fishing, we've got it all here
Just sit and relax while you drink down a beer

You do fancy fishing?
Cost ya five-fifty
Could catch a couple
Isn't that nifty?

Wanna fish on the lake?
We'll rent you a boat
But when it fills up with rain
I hope you can float

Come on up
Now hurry, honey
Come on up
And bring your money

Come to Canada
Where lakes are blue
Come to Canada
It's right for you.

1977

AM I A RAIN MAN?

We're a good way down our separate roads
With no friends around to ease our loads
The burden is big of that we're sure
Please help us dig so we may endure

The future looks bright then suddenly dim
As dark as night without a whim
I'm sure you know why it's always the same
'Cause wherever I go, it's gonna rain

Am I a rain man?
Or should I ask,
Am I a sane man
Behind this mask?
Will I wash away your worry?
Your troubles of the day?
You had better hurry
What more can I say?
Get away! Get away!

I bring the showers – I cause the pain
Wherever I go, you know it's gonna rain
The thunder will roar and lightning strikes too
Please close your door or I'll get you!
Bright bolts from the air will surely take form
If I'm merely there, I'll bring on the storm

I could flood your home – I could flood your town
Wherever I roam, I'll bring the rain down
I don't want to take no bus or train
Wherever I go, it's gonna rain

Am I a rain man?
Or should I ask,
Am I a sane man
Behind this mask?

1977

56

ARRIVAL AND DEPARTURE II

So we'd been rained out and decided to go
We turned about and really felt low
We rolled up the tents and put out the fire
It didn't make sense; the ground wasn't drier

With Jim at the wheel, we made it back
Had a good meal then hit the sack
The very next day we recorded some songs
In our own special way though we knew they were wrong

From "Live Means to Live" to the Beatles' "Get Back"
We had to give; it was time to pack
We stuffed everything in that little trunk
It lost its spring 'cause it really sunk

We stayed up all night; ghost stories were told
To give us a fright and the wind was so cold
We had music too on the player down there
What more to do than to go down the stairs

The basement was dark and in some places wet
There wasn't a mark, but I wouldn't forget
We finally went to sleep as the sun began to rise
Mine wasn't deep, but I closed my eyes

We all were alive just two hours later
It was my turn to drive
We were off for greater...

1977

LIKE FOOLS IN THE HILLS

...places and different faces that haven't been seen before
We drove very far in that little car and sometimes stopped at a store
We bought some lunch so we could munch along the way
The towns were hick and the ride seemed quick though it took all day
The Badlands were all right
It was a different sight than I had ever seen
So soon we departed for we had only started, if you know what I mean
We finally made it there and I could only stare at the forest of green
It was beautiful to behold
As great as I was told and greater than I'd seen
We stayed in Deadwood and things were looking good
From our hotel room so high
We needed to use our feet so we went out to eat
But the prices were so high
For those who would arrive, Deadwood came alive that Saturday night
Some people got mad and we were glad that we were out of sight

We left the Franklin the next day
We had to be on our way to the 1880 train
The five of us climbed aboard and if the engine had roared
You know that there'd be rain
On the road past a beautiful lake
We knew that it would take us to the mountain of Crazy Horse
Though not really much to see
We knew that it would be for those who will take this course
Onward to Bedrock City which was far from being pretty
Maybe we shouldn't have been there
Leon and Jim felt it was silly, but Paul, Scott and I really
Didn't seem to care
So we went across the street and we were soon to meet a horse owner
It was up to us to decide if we really wanted to ride
And you know, there wasn't a groaner
So we all hopped on and even Leon was able to come along
We rode the trail and I was the tail so I sang a song
It was an hour of the day we all thought was okay
But wasn't really too hot
Next we saw the dogs of the prairie
And discovered it was very hard to get a shot

It was very warm with no sight of a storm as we entered Wind Cave
It was cool down there which was only fair considering what we gave
We'd had a busy day and so we decided to stay in Custer for the night
We'd all been fed so we flipped for the bed which I won without a fight

At last the great day was here
It was beautiful and clear that Fourth of July
We went to see the mountain
Which seemed to be a fountain of heads that could fly
Brave and bold they seemed
I had never dreamed it would be like this
Their heads were in the sky
They had caught my eye
This I couldn't miss
The flags from every state
Were hanging there just great along the walkway
Of the gifts we had bought, the room we had not, but they fit anyway
By Rushmore Cave we'd gone soft
And were all ripped off except for Jim
He'd seen it before and so he stayed in the store
I wished that I'd been him

Rapid City was the end of the line and our wallets were far from fine
Screaming from loss and pain
Went to see a porpoise show, but it was "no go"
'cause I had brought the rain
The porpoise wouldn't perform because I had brought the storm
So we went out to eat again
After McDonald's, it was off to the races
Dog instead of horse faces which was about to begin
We were all out of luck
It seemed we'd paid our last buck for that final motel room
Each of us took a shower and within the next hour
Darkness filled the room

Early the next morning, Cosmos was a warning for us to leave
So after a stop at a base, we left that whole place of make believe
So on the way to Wall, I felt that all of us had our thrills
Like five-sided dice, we'd paid the price like fools in the hills.

1977

LIVING IN THE PAST

Living in the past is not all that great
For we all know it's much more than fate
That brings us together on that certain date in time

You see, I can tell you, I've lived in the past
All friends and lovers have grown up too fast
It makes me cry 'cause I want it to last forever

The greatest of friends have all up and gone
Me and the others are still going on
With even some news ones like Kevin and John
To have some laughs with

Off to the movie; it's always the late show
The whole gang comes whenever we go
Two crowded cars and the sun's getting low in the sky again

Whether it's "Jaws", "The Deep" or the great "Star Wars"
Somehow we manage to get in those doors
Only to walk on those same dirty floors as we've always done

Yes, living in the past is full of good times
As long as you've got the quarters and dimes
So why am I making up all of these rhymes for you to read?

I'm here to tell you, you can never go back
You see, the old times are gone like a sack
And if you try, it's wisdom you lack just like me.

1977

I'M JUST A SAD MAN

A lot of things I dream up
Everyone sings; we team up
"Kirk to Enterprise—let's beam up"

I was the ad man
I never get mad, man
I'm just a sad man

Don't wake me, I'm sleepy
Don't shake me, I'm weepy
For God's sake, Me
I'm creepy!

I was the ad man
Not like my Dad, man
I'm just a sad man

Yes, I lost my lover
Was never really there
Thought I was above her
With her long dark hair
But it was just a cover
We could never share

I was the ad man
I blew it bad, man
I'm just a sad man.

1977

AM I A RAIN MAN? (REPRISE)

Raindrops tapping on your window
Calling you, each one
Come closer and listen
Don't leave until they're done

They're trying to make you understand
But you're just a common man
It's up to you to conceive
A plan for all, if you believe

The constant cloud follows me
It shadows and wets my head
Is it something I can't see
Or something I've done instead?

The skies are clearing now
The sun is going to shine
But when another shower comes
Is it really mine?

Am I a rain man?
Or should I ask,
Am I a sane man
Behind this mask?

1977

EPILOGUE: HOME IS THE HERO

Home is the hero
He's come back at last
From the land of his friends
From the land of his past
Yes, the vacation is over
His time has expired
Gone are the laughs and the loves
And all he desired
He has touched that portion of time
And it seems to be said
He should never think to go back
To that voice in his head:

"Come on up
Now hurry, honey
Come on up and bring your money
Come to Canada
Where lakes are blue
Come to Canada
It's right for you"

This past is all but forgotten
It hurts to remember
But he knows he must look ahead
With force although tender
With the passing of days and weeks
The deadline draws near
He has all the time to decide
But the paths are unclear
With arrivals and departures all coming and going
It's hard for him to settle down and make a good showing
He knows the loneliness has passed, but the rain still comes down
He must concentrate his efforts with his sight and his sound
Yes, home is the hero for all he is worth
If he tries hard, he can make it
On this planet called Earth.

1977

FUN AND FANCY

WE'RE GOING TO THE MATH LAB

WHEN THE WEATHER IS COLD

ATHENS TOWN

J.R. EWING

LIONEL'S VINYL

CARLTON THE RED SOX CATCHER

EVERYWHERE IT'S CHRISTMAS TIME

HEADLIGHTERS

WE ARE THE SCOUTS!

JOE'S SONG

WE'RE GOING TO THE MATH LAB

We're gonna have a test and we don't want to goof
We're gonna try our best to work that proof
We gotta multiply; we're supposed to make a graph
And with circles use pi but all we do is laugh

We're going to the Math Lab
Yeah, we're going to the Math Lab
We're gonna learn to add in the Math Lab
When we're in the Math Lab

We can work it out; it's on the other side
If we change it about just use it to divide
Say, there's Mister K and he's coming this way
And I think he's gonna say
"Where's your homework for today?"

It's in the Math Lab
Yeah, we did it in the Math Lab
We're gonna learn to add in the Math Lab
When we're in the Math Lab

Well, we took the test but I think I failed mine
Though I tried my best, I forgot the cosine
I left it in the Math Lab
Yeah, we're going to the Math Lab

Problem number four had a big exponent
Didn't see it before and I wish I'd known it
In the Math Lab
Yeah, we're going to the Math Lab
We're gonna learn to add in the Math Lab
When we're in the Math Lab

Quadrants and rays and sets and triangles
Slopes and formulas and factors...

1976

WHEN THE WEATHER IS COLD

When the weather is hot I smell the things that start to rot
I can't figure out where I'm not when the weather is hot

When the weather is warm I see the clouds that start the storm
I may get wet, but I'm still in form when the weather is warm

When the weather is fair I lay back without a care
And watch the birds fly thru the air when the weather is fair

When the weather is cool I always seem to be in school
I can't think; I'm such a fool when the weather is cool

But when the weather is cold
The snow comes down and takes right hold

My blood freezes when I go outside
My eyes are frozen; they're open wide

The cursed cold is a villain indeed
His disguise is white, but pay no heed

He'll attack at dawn or worse at night
He'll steal your limbs and even your sight

You can't defeat this powerful foe
If you try, he'll only snow

He'll cover your home, your car and street
He'll trap you inside with your heat

So stay inside whenever it snows
Or even worse, whenever it blows

The cold has a friend for which he'll send
Perhaps you've felt, he's called the wind

The wind blows the snow over the highway
When I get home, it's in the driveway

Your lips, he'll chap; your face, he'll burn
You're frozen to the ground with nowhere to turn

Just the cold himself is terrible
With the chill factor, unbearable

Freezing you solid until you are numb
Worst are your toes, fingers and thumbs

Men tremble and shake whenever they hear
"Winter is coming; it's that time of year"

Just look around and you can tell
We're living in a frozen hell

It's death to the skin, but pleasing to the sight
It's that white world of winter, flu and frostbite

It saps your life and you'll grow old
When the weather is cold.

1977

ATHENS TOWN

Let's all go down to Athens Town
Everyone around loves to dig the sound
Let's all get drunk at the Mad Hatter
We'll fail our tests but it doesn't matter

Come and meet people in this wild, wild place
Just park your car if you can find a space
Let's all go down to Athens Town
Everyone around loves to dig the sound

See you Saturday to watch some football
Just be sure to say, "Hi Y'all!"
Have a good time in this crazy college town
You act so stupid, you silly foolish clown

Let's all go down to Athens Town
Everyone around loves to dig the sound
Let's all go down to Athens Town.

1979

J.R. EWING

J.R. Ewing has the best oil around
He handles his business very carefully and we know him well
He's the man we all love to hate on our television screens

J.R. Ewing was shot last season
But he's still up and around
He's a man of great logic and reason
And that's why he's king of Dallas town

J.R. Ewing, what happened to you?
You were on "I Dream of Jeannie"
You were such a nice Air Force major
But now you're nothing but a meanie

J.R. Ewing lives at Southfork ranch
With the rest of his kin and clan
Bobby, Pam, Ray and Lucy
Oh, how they despise this man

J.R. Ewing has the best oil around
He handles his business very carefully and we know him well

J.R. Ewing was shot last season
But he's still up and around
He's a man of great logic and reason
And that's why he's king of Dallas town!

1980

LIONEL'S VINYL

There once was a music lover named Lionel
Whose record collection was final
Then along came CD's
To his ears did they please
Now what does he do with the vinyl?

1985

CARLTON THE RED SOX CATCHER

Carlton the Red Sox catcher swung a very might bat
Because when it came to hitting
He was very good at that

All of the fans in Boston used to love to scream and shout
Runners that tried for second
Carlton quickly threw them out

In the sixth World Series game
Carlton came to bat you know
Carlton hit the ball so high
Red Sox fans let out a cry!

All of the other Red Sox knew that Carlton won the game
They lost the Series that year
But they never felt ashamed

Fred, Jim, Yaz and Evans
Really could hit that ball
They love to play in Fenway
With the Big Green Monster wall

In the sixth World Series game
Carlton came to bat you know
Carlton hit the ball so high
Red Sox fans let out a cry!

All of the fans in Boston used to love to scream and shout
Runners that tried for second
Carlton quickly threw them out

Carlton the Red Sox catcher swung a very might bat
Because when it came to hitting
He was very good at that

We love Carlton Fisk – yeah!

1980

EVERYWHERE IT'S CHRISTMAS TIME

I met a fat man on the street last night
In his teeth a pipe held tight
Blowing rings of smoke around his head
And this is what he said:

"You'd better watch out
You'd better not cry
You'd better not pout"
So I asked him, "Why?"

He said his name was Santa
And he was coming to Atlanta
To bring lots of toys
To all the girls and boys

He said it's time again for Christmas
And he didn't want to miss us

He'd come to watch our spirits grow
Seeing happy folks hanging mistletoe
Feeling children's smiles that really glow
But I pointed out, "We have no snow"

I said, "It's hard to get into the spirit of the season
Without snow on the ground, we have no reason
To hold such joy on that silent night
I wish there was some way to make Christmas white!"

But Santa said, "The South has snow
Just look around and you'll see it's so
Snow isn't always that stuff from the sky
Snow is the love your heart holds inside"

Pure snow is the peace we all share
Deep in your heart, I know that it's there
Clean as can be for those who you care
For friends and lovers and all that is fair

Now I know that everywhere it's Christmas time
Everywhere it's Christmas time
And if you believe that you'll truly see
Then I wish you'd all join and sing with me:

Everywhere it's Christmas time
From the far east to the west
People praying to the Lord
As young return to the nest

Everywhere it's Christmas time
As the snow begins to fall
Family fun is here again
While love shines on us all

Everywhere it's Christmas time
Everywhere it's Christmas time
Lighted candles really shine
Everywhere at Christmas time

Everywhere it's Christmas time
From the far east to the west
People praying to the Lord
Please make this one the best

Everywhere it's Christmas time
As the snow begins to fall
Family fun is here again
While love shines on us all

Family fun is here again
While love shines on us all

Yes, family fun is here again
While love...shines...on...us...all!

1979

HEADLIGHTERS

We're driving down the highway; it's late at night
We're looking up ahead, but something's not right
There's a car coming with one beam of light
The other one is out, limiting his sight
When he gets closer, tell you what to do
We gotta let him know he's not getting through
Without a little warning from only me and you
He's gonna see our lights; he'll wish he had two

We're driving down the road; it's well after dark
We're looking up ahead; cruising like a shark
We keep our eyes open as we pass the park
Then we turn the corner and I yell to Mark:
"There's a one-eye coming the other way
His left light is black; his right a single ray"
When he gets closer, we're gonna make him pay
Now we start to flicker; he can't get away

We're the Headlighters; we're looking for you
We're the Headlighters; our aim is true
Flash our high beams right in your face
You'd better get it replaced!

We're driving down the street underneath the stars
We're looking up ahead watching all the cars
Always changing lanes; breezing by the bars
Then we spot a fiend; he won't get very far
The cops don't even care, but we know it isn't right
To drive after dark with only one light
So we'll do our share each and every night
If you've got one out then you'll see our brights!

We're the Headlighters; we're looking for you
We're the Headlighters; our aim is true
Flash our high beams right in your face
You'd better get it replaced!

1985

WE ARE THE SCOUTS!

Scouts!
We are the Scouts
May no one ever have any doubts
We can get the job done 'cause we're number one!
We are the Scouts
We are the Scouts!

Planning and fanning – burning and learning
Hiking and biking – rowing and going
Sending and mending
Is what we do and there's always something new in the Scouts
We are the Scouts!

Scouts!
To be a Scout is to know what it is all about
You can learn to stop a bleeder and then become a leader in the Scouts
We are the Scouts!

Scouts!
To know a Scout
You can tell by the way we sing and shout
We work out in the sun but we're always having fun in the Scouts
We are the Scouts!

Camping and cramping – grinning and winning
Knowing and showing – swimming and trimming
Dishing and fishing
Is what we do and there's always something new in the Scouts
We are the Scouts!

Scouts!
We are the Scouts
May no one ever have any doubts
As we march on down the trail
We know that we will never fail in the Scouts
We are the Scouts!

1978

JOE'S SONG

Rock and Roll won't save your soul
The music's great, but it takes its toll
Be careful now—don't lose control
Worship Jesus, not Rock and Roll.

1989

CLOUDS OF CONFUSION

THROUGH THE EYES OF ONE

As I gaze with eyes ablaze
Staring up at the skies
It makes me think to find the link
Before this green world dies

Any place that one can face
One can surely tell
The people there, they have no care
So they all start to yell

Say, it's the same way every day
Everywhere I see
It pains me too to think of you
Lost in this crowded sea

Living here with all this fear
Is not for you nor I
And so I say we must get away
Before we begin to die

I see it's bad and it makes me sad
And I know it makes you blue
But that's the way and it's the price we pay
To start the world anew.

1976

CROSS TOWN

Half from the west side
Half from the east
Some drive the most
While some drive the least

Crippled carburetors and turning tires
Painting pictures with pairs of pliers
Multicolored rivers flow back and forth
East to west and south to north

Cross Town's not so far away
Looking for a place to stay
Right and left then up and down
Point the way to Cross Town

Gray skies crying through clouds of confusion
What is the meaning of this intrusion?
Are we all about to lose our minds?
We can't escape our daily grinds

Another day of morning drives
Merely existing; complacent lives
Who can save that which survives?
While outside a thunderstorm thrives

Cross Town shines not far from here
Illuminating images of illicit fear
Exercise caution, don't you know
Or else all things will start to glow

Purple, red and tangerine
Yellow, gold and even green
So many colors our eyes do see
Chasing rainbows eagerly

All men aggravate allergies
Dust and smoke and fallen leaves
Everyone needs to be where they're not
Going Cross Town is what they're taught

Cross Town's not so far away
Looking for a place to stay
Right and left then up and down
Point the way to Cross Town

A Moonie sells flowers on an exit ramp
A scientist studies a postage stamp
So many interpersonal communications
Adjusting to life's situations

Going Cross Town can leave you crazy
Left alone, but never lazy
Prevailing priorities press your pride
Utter frustration you feel inside

Cross Town's not so far away
Looking for a place to stay
Right and left then up and down
Point the way to Cross Town.

1986

LIFE MEANS TO LIVE

In the world today we pretend to see
Things in a way they weren't meant to be—oh no
On our tubes today we watch and listen
To what it has to say, but the point we're missin' is...

Life means to live
Yeah—life means to live
You got to give
If life is to live

That ain't no slip
Don't give me no lip!
You know it's true
I wouldn't jive you

In the world today you're gonna see
Things in the way they were meant to be—oh yeah
And on the radio you're gonna hear
The greatest rock show ever put in tenth gear—yeah!

And of course everyone's bringin'
Many mouths to do the singin'
Everybody's pitching in and givin'
And life goes right on livin'—'cause...

Life means to live
Yeah—life means to live
You gotta give
If life is to live—yeah!

Life means to live
Life means to live
Life means to live...

1976

THINK ALL DAY

You know we think all day
Yes, yes we think all day
But don't you turn away
'Cause we've been led astray

You know we think all day
We look up to our R.A.
He's got a 4.0
He doesn't want to blow

Never been out to Hollywood
Never seen a movie star
Success never tasted so good
Study and you'll go far

You know we think all day
And we swing all night
Everything's right or wrong
Or it's black or white
Is it wrong or right?

That's why we think all day
Hey, hey we think all day
But don't you turn away
'Cause we've been led astray

Never been out to Hollywood
Never traveled in the month of May
Even though we wish we could
We still sit and think all day.

1979

I CAN'T BELIEVE IT

Everybody's screaming about equal rights, sex and discrimination
Yelling, fighting, can't get along, yet you call it "civilization"
I can't believe it, oo!
You know I can't believe it, oo!
If it just don't fit, I can't believe it
I can't believe it, oo!

We got terrorists, rapists, killers galore
Making this world a mess
And nobody ever does nothing about it
C'mon World, confess!
Well, Jimmy tries to make some peace, but he sells them planes instead
If that's the way that peace is made, we're all gonna end up dead
I can't believe it, oo!
You know I can't believe it, oo!
If it just don't fit, I can't believe it
I can't believe it, oo!

We got criminals in cars, drunks in bars, drug addicts getting high
Everything from wife beaters to junk food eaters
All I ask is "Why?"
Some people go out on strike to get some better pay
But when it drags on for way too long, this is what I say:
I can't believe it, oo!
You know I can't believe it, oo!
If it just don't fit, I can't believe it
I can't believe it, oo!

We got problems in the ocean; problems on land
And all that crap falling out of the sky
Got inflation, welfare and assassination
Lord, it makes me cry
I can't believe it, oo!
You know I can't believe it, oo!
If it just don't fit, I can't believe it
I can't believe it at all.

1978

IN ONE EAR AND OUT THE OTHER

Political nonsense in the air
Promises that aren't really there
Candidates on the campaign trail
Policies that can only fail

Hostages being held for a year
The day of their release draws near
Do you really have a say when you vote on Election Day?

Please show me a sign
That will change my mind
To bring hope and faith to my brother

Life has only been tasted
Though so much has been wasted
By going in one ear and out the other

We watch football from the stands
Then we listen to the bands
Who play their hearts out for each other

But it matters not who plays on these sunny Saturdays
It all goes in one ear and out the other

Our team is high in the polls
Getting bids from major bowls
Hoping they will be number one
After all is said and done

As the years go by I've come to know
They pass by faster as they go
And the memories will follow one another

So the information is lost
And the time and the cost
Has gone in one ear and out the other.

1980

DEPRESSION

It was a world of black and white
The dust was so thick it seemed like night
People did what they thought was right
Dying of hunger, no strength to fight

Hear from the past their long loud cries
Failure after failure; so many tries
Wiping the dust and the dirt from their eyes
They all lie down; everyone dies.

1977

GONE

I have traveled much too far

Holding the world up like a jar
And all the people fall off and fly
Then land on the sun; why don't they fry?
Even the stars are laughing at me

Now in the cars, I hope they will see
Over the blackness past the farms
Running to catch them with my arms
They all hate me; oh drat!
How I hate the bugs that go splat

Driving me on to reach my goal
All I want is to crawl in a hole
Know you this before I leave
Onward they come and deceive
They'll mix your mind and soul as well
And take you on a trip through Hell.

1977

VEHEMENT COMES TO SERENITY

It was a small town
Somewhere, someplace on the ground
This town, it matters not where
Be it here or be it there

It was a very tranquil place
Everyone wore a smiling face
It is here our story begins
Somewhat different from the way it ends

Mr. Rogers had just closed his store
Walked outside, turned and shut the door
Dr. Wilson was in a happy way
Had not one single accident this day

Mrs. Parker was having a drink; it was hot
Of alcoholic beverages they had heard not
And what of a cigarette to smoke?
These people did not want to cough and choke

Every Saturday was the baseball game
Each team had spirit in its name
It was Serenity East and Serenity West
To see for that week who was the best

And when the game was done
Upon the setting sun
It mattered not who won
Just as long as it was fun

And of course it always was
Everyone knows why, just because
And when they looked above
They would see a bird, a dove

Yes, this is how it was, everyone could see
The faces of their friends were always happy
But all this was in the past
It is sad it did not last

Zach Vehement came to town one day
And he did things in a different way
He brought with him barrels of beer
And told the people they had nothing to fear

He gave them tobacco to smoke
And said bad health was just a joke
But worst of all, he brought them the gun
And told them it was the only way to have fun

The people became less innocuous since that night
And thought it would be fun to hurt and fight
So that Saturday there was no ball game
Since Zach came it never was the same

People attacked no matter the weather
Just to prove who was the better
Then gunfire split the air
And the town died then and there

When it was over, Zach came out
He looked around and about
Then he glanced up above
And noticed the crying of the dove

He fired a shot and killed it
And it fell into a baseball mitt
Then Zach left pleased and fine
To kill another town, perhaps yours or mine.

1976

THE RETURN OF THE EAGLE

He claws and scratches sandy ground
With feathered arms, he crawls around
Then strains to stand upon the mound

His eyes look up to windy skies
He spreads his weathered wings and tries
And like the bird he is, he flies.

1977

BROWN PAPER BAG

You had so much to learn in such a short time
A recycled decoupage from the processing line
And you know very little but you try very hard
And you're open to the world as you reach for a star
And your life is lived in a brown paper bag
You're an empty jar without a price tag

Bread, cans, produce and steak really make our bodies ache
Bagging is no piece of cake, it's all up to what you make
From across the country food is shipped
Carts fall over when you've tripped
You smile inside when you've been tipped
Unless of course you've been ripped

Soon you're filled to the limit for you hold all you can
They say that you're worthy; they say you're a man
But they still increase the burden
For they'll give more than take
Until your seams begin to burst
For then it's much too late
And your life is lived in a brown paper bag
You're an empty jar without a price tag

Working around you are various kinds
From ROTCs to rookies and those with no minds
People fall in the long checkout lines
We've all gone through this too many times
Behind our counters we work all day
For the supervisors we must pay
It always works this way
And in the eyes of a redcoat we have no say

So they've ripped through your soul and you bow out with grace
You're just an empty shell allied with empty space
And your life is lived in a brown paper bag
You're a nameless man without a price tag.

1977

SEPARATE ROADS

Left two years ago but never slipped away
Voices kept us close just like yesterday.
Now I've left the homeland
Perhaps never to return
Will my friends remember me?
This I hope to learn.
He's the oldest of them all
Now drives a fancy car
Only I can understand the reason he'll go far.
Dark and quiet is this next one
But normal in his way
Just read his words and you'll agree that he has much to say.
From a language to the sciences
He explained it all
So that I might make it over the learning wall.

It's separate roads we follow
It's separate paths we take
We're heading for tomorrow
The future we will make

He's neatness and order personified
Perfection is his goal
The Academy will teach him how to use his mind and soul.
This one is observant
He can see right through your eyes
Clever although cautious
He needs no second tries.
Usually the easy-going type
Works just to earn his share
But looks ahead for things to come and adventures he will dare.

It's separate roads we follow
It's separate lives we've laid
The future holds no sorrow
For these friends I've made.

1977

PEACE IS

Peace is the tenderness of touch
Peace is the feeling of loving so much
Peace is the warmth of a lover's lips
Peace is the feeling from the neck to the hips

Peace can be death or eternal life
Peace is when man calls woman his wife
Peace can be sleeping, but never alone
Peace is release in writing a poem

Peace is music both soft and loud
Peace is the rain that falls from the cloud
Peace is the smile on anyone's face
Peace is to work at your own pace

Peace is the happiness you've shared
Peace is everlasting to show that you cared
Peace is in God who cannot deceive
Peace is in Heaven for those who believe

Peace is understanding of your fellow man
Peace is the power to show that you can
Peace is togetherness and cooperation
Peace is for all of this generation

Peace is all this and so much more
Peace is the mind that's willing to soar
Peace is for us, for me and for you
Peace is for the silent, the wise and the true

Peace is for all, when all are one
Peace is eternal and will never be done
But most of all, peace is love
And love is the thing there's too little of.

1977

FRIDAY NIGHTS (LONELY TREE)

Friday nights at Little King's
That's where the jukebox sings
Play a song from long ago or the theme from a picture show
(Take out a quarter and let it go)

"Lonely tree
Only you can comfort me
Here I am, so let me see
Your life, oh lonely tree

On any night
You are such a lovely sight
Please tell me now if I am right
Oh lonely tree, on any night

I just can't decide so I cried
It couldn't be
Now it's much too late so my fate
Rests on lonely tree

Lonely tree
Now that you have set me free
No one else will ever see
Your life, oh lonely tree

Dee dee dee dee, dee dee-dee"

Some songs are good and some are great
Like that sandwich I just ate
Let's get in line and buy another
Take one home for my mother

Some people think we do strange things
On Friday nights at Little King's
But good times are all we seek
We'll be back again next week.

1977

PHANTOM NEIGHBORS

Who's that? (Don't know); Could it be next door?
Strange noises last night (Sounded like a fight)
Never see anyone, in or out or on the run
Mysterious shadows blend into the night
Never see them in broad daylight
But I'll keep looking for them to appear
Even if I wait for the rest of the year
My name is Arthur and this is my home
I live with my wife, but we're not alone
We bought this house nearly four years ago
We wanted some quiet, not a creep show
We hear these strange noises from the house next door
Weird conversations which we can't ignore
The Wilsons moved out nearly two months ago
So who is it talking behind that window?

It's the Phantom Neighbors of Lonelybrook Lane
Specters and ghosts which we cannot explain
Nocturnal noises into the night; skulking shadows that slip out of sight

That house has been vacant for nearly nine weeks
Now it's beginning to give us the creeps
If someone moved in then we must have been out
Visiting friends or driving about
My name is Arthur and I'm in distress
1201 Lonelybrook is my address
The voices next door I can't understand
Talk about money and making a plan
Perhaps some type of business providing a service
I don't know what kind but it makes me nervous
Illegal deals are done with unusual style
Who else would keep such a low profile?

It's the Phantom Neighbors of Lonelybrook Lane
Specters and ghosts which we cannot explain
Nocturnal noises into the night; skulking shadows that slip out of sight.

1988

FALLING THRU AN HOURGLASS

He was just a little boy playing with his little toy
Until the day his best friend Roy taught him how to destroy
Then he had his ups and downs in his travels thru cities and towns
Growing up with all the sounds
His face has since worn many frowns
So he's falling thru an hourglass
Falling thru an hourglass
Hoping that the pain will pass
Falling thru an hourglass

He was trying to understand the music made by the band
But it just slipped thru his hand much like granules made of sand
He blamed it all on the government
They told him how his money was spent
It went to pay the poor people's rent
And now no one knows where he went
You see he's falling thru an hourglass
Falling thru an hourglass
Hoping that the pain will pass
Falling thru an hourglass

Never had he known so much gloom than when he hid in his little room
It became his eternal tomb for he had fallen to his doom
All he wanted was a little more time
To try and make the end words rhyme
And if he showed you just the smallest sign
Then he must have reached the end of the line
'Cause he's falling thru an hourglass
Falling thru an hourglass
Along with the rest of the class
Falling thru an hourglass

Falling thru an hourglass
Falling thru an hourglass
Hoping that the pain will pass
Falling thru an hourglass.

1977

EIGHTEEN YEARS OLD

Suddenly you've realized that your childhood is gone
Lost now forever; you've got to move on
Eighteen years old – you ain't just a kid
You want to go back and do the things that you did

You're just out of school and life is now waiting
You've got to live it and get a good rating
Eighteen years old and it's no longer fun
Now you're responsible for the things that you've done

You've got to do something so you give them your name
Say goodbye to the family – it'll never be the same
(No, it's never the same again)

Eighteen years old and you're still catching cold
Still getting gray by the day
Eighteen years old – your body is sold
You've just seen the light in the night

Eighteen years old – they call you a man
But there are things in this world that you don't understand
Still you know a lot now
You've opened some doors
But if you plan to make it you've got to know more

Eighteen years old – go out and vote
Choose the less of two evils and don't miss the boat
Life moves too fast
We all get behind
Don't let it trouble you
Just take your time

Eighteen years old and you're still catching cold
Still getting gray by the day
Eighteen years old – your body is sold
You've just seen the light in the night.

1978

AT 21

At 21, I've seen the sun
I don't catch rays, but I still have fun
I've been over that hill a time or two
And what I've seen just ain't true

I'm looking for my special lady
A gorgeous girl not a Sexy Sadie
I've known plenty of girls that weren't my type
I'll pick one out when the time is ripe

Yeah—so give me a chance to show what I've done
Clear the clouds from the shining sun
It's time to pull out my gambling gun
'Cause life's more fun at 21

A lot of folks will go out and drink
I don't do that 'cause it's hard to think
And I don't go to parties 'cause they're such a drag
I'd rather put tape on a comic bag

Baseball's always been my favorite game
Football's all right, but it's not the same
Everybody asks "Who shot J.R.?"
I don't know, but it made him a star

Yeah—so give me a chance to show what I've done
Clear the clouds from the shining sun
It's time to pull out my gambling gun
'Cause life's more fun at 21

"Where are you from?" they all ask me
I tell them I was born in Mississippi
But that doesn't mean I know it well
'Cause I moved from there to the frozen hell

Where the wind is so wild it'll blow you away
And make you believe in yesterday
Although I've lived all over the place
My mind still dreams of outer space

Yeah—so give me a chance to show what I've done
Clear the clouds from the shining sun
It's time to pull out my gambling gun
'Cause life's more fun at 21

Going to school has been my way of life
Most come here to meet their wife
I'm more concerned with getting a job
It's better to work than to steal or rob

I'd love to sit around and tell you more
But I'm afraid I'd become a bore
So I'll just sing the chorus again
And I'd be happy if ya'll would join in

Yeah—so give me a chance to show what I've done
Clear the clouds from the shining sun
It's time to pull out my gambling gun
'Cause life's more fun at 21.

1980

PRIME-TIME TELEVISION

Prime-time television
I'm on prime-time television
And you've seen my face on your picture screen before
Prime-time television
I'm on prime-time television
But I've been misplaced; I'm not in your scene anymore

I play a good-guy cowboy on this shoot-em-up western show
And I ride into the sunset as the credits roll
I'm riding high in the saddle; fastest gun in the west
I've got the greatest time slot; my ratings are the best
I get to do commercials; I've been in the magazines
"People," "Us" and "Newsweek" really dig my scenes

They said they'd make me famous and I reckon that's what they did
People come from miles away for a chance to meet "the Kid"
You know I'm making lots of money; more than you've ever seen
I go for rides all over in the back of my limousine

But you said you wouldn't have me
No, you didn't want to
If there's one thing that I've got to have
Then Lord, it must be you

I could never figure out what's wrong with me
I try to be a real nice guy
But I must be missing something 'cause I never caught your eye
I'm not a Clint Eastwood; I'm not even a Little Joe
I'm just a good-guy cowboy on this shoot-em-up western show

Prime-time television
I'm on prime-time television
And you've seen my face on your picture screen before
Prime-time television
I'm on prime-time television
But I've been misplaced; I'm not in your scene anymore.

1982

TURTLE BLOOD

The road grew ever darker and dim
The world was much smaller to him
Still the question to the answer was unknown
His mind and his body were full grown

From the lake it crawled up into the grass
Its eyes were little pieces of glass
It left behind its swampy cell
But it could never escape its muddy shell

He continued to travel and think his life
Wishing to cut loose with a knife
After days of looking thru his windshield
He stopped to work in a field

Each day brought many different scenes
And one day it hid within the beans
It was happy with the new home it had made
But homes are destroyed by the blade

The blade cut deep and threw it out
Ousted in pain without a shout
The turtle blood was splashed upon his shoe
And he knew...

Oh, the question to the answer was "Where?"
And all he could do was simply stare
His direction had finally been found
It lay there bleeding on the ground

It probably died there that day
But he'll keep on making his way
He may not have crawled out of mud
But within his veins flows that turtle blood.

1978

CREATURE OF HABIT

I never do anything different
It's the same thing everyday
Pants on first then pullover shirt
To me it's the only way
The Earth turns green only once a year and the sun will come and go
They are the river of forever and I'm just part of the flow
I'm just a creature of habit
Always keep it clean
Never stray from the middle of the road and follow the same routine

Cruising down the same path
It's just my way of life
But everyone comes to that fork in the road
Stay single or take a wife?
Family patterns are costly
It's all in the cards they say
You can put it off now, but you must make the choice someday

Creature of habit
You may never find your queen
Don't ever take any chances
Follow the same routine
To me it's extremely important to always be on time
Failing to keep an appointment is just like committing a crime
Things must be taken in order; consistency is the key
Man and machine fused together; I'm not really sure which is me

Creature of habit
Saw you in the magazine
Impressions are intangible
So follow the same routine
Creature of habit
Remember what you've seen
Return to your tomorrows
And follow the same routine
And follow the same routine and follow the same routine...

1979

RAINBOW'S END

At a rainbow's end, take a look around
That's what I've been told
At a rainbow's end, dig a hole in the ground
To find your pot of gold
Everywhere there's rainbows stretched across the skies
An arc of many colors right before your eyes

At the daylight's end, there's a thunderstorm
The rain comes pouring down
At the shower's end, a rainbow is born
From the sunshine all around
Take me to the rainbow's end
Take me there my lifetime friend
Show me all there is to see
Show me all there is to be

Your day is so bright when you are first born
So carefree and innocent, but then comes the storm
Your day is so dark and depression sets in
The clouds of confusion
Where to begin?

Take me to the rainbow's end
Take me there my trusted friend
Show me all there is to see
Show me all there is to be
At the daylight's end, there's a thunderstorm
The rain comes pouring down
At the shower's end, a rainbow is born
From the sunshine all around
Everywhere there's rainbows stretched across the skies
An arc of many colors right before your eyes
At a lifetime's end, take a look behind
To see what you have done
At a lifetime's end, have peace of mind
You've only just begun.

1987

NOW HERE COME THE FULL MOON!

HE'S A WEREWOLF

CLASSICS OF HORROR

THE DEATH OF THE DARK DEMON

THE FATE OF THE WEREWOLF

HAUNTED HALLOWEEN

HE'S A WEREWOLF

His name is Michael
He's been acting so strangely
Since he became eighteen
Now they're grossly mangled
He kill you, me very soon
His claws are so deadly now here come the full moon!

He's a werewolf
(Ah-woo!)
Werewolf Man

Her name is Cindy
She fell in love with Michael
She's been very worried
Since the lunar cycle
He kill two, three every night
When the full moon is out their blood bleeds so bright!

He's a werewolf
(Ah-woo!)
Werewolf Man

She's found a rifle
She's seen "Kolchak: Night Stalker"
She has silver bullets
Now she's the street walker
He kill Sue, Lee before 10:00
Cindy sees Michael and points the gun at him!

He's a werewolf
(Shoot him!)
Cindy did.

1979

CLASSICS OF HORROR

By the end of 1931, the horror had only begun
When Dracula spoke, we held our breath
"There are far worse things awaiting man than death"
Less we forget Lugosi's famous line, "I never drink wine"

Frankenstein's Monster made many afraid
"The brain of a dead man waiting to live again in a body I made"
He worked on the creature for many days
"I made it with my own hands with the bodies I took from graves"
"Look, no blood, no decay. Just a few stitches"
"Let's have one final test. Throw the switches"
And who could forget the words of Colin Clive?
"It's alive! It's alive! It's alive!"

In "The Mummy" the horror became worse
"Good heavens, what a terrible curse!"
He came to life in that ancient place
"You should have seen his face!"
Imhotep spoke from on high
"You also know that you must return that scroll to me or die"
Van Sloan knew that the Mummy's power never ceases
"If I could get my hands on you, I'd break your dried flesh to pieces!"

"The walls around are bare
Echoing to our laughter
As though the dead were there"

Although Dracula always got the girl
"An Invisible Man can rule the world!"
A few chemicals mixed together every day
"And flesh and blood and bone just fade away!"
Pretorius' vision was Frankenstein's fate
"Now together we will create his mate"
The Monster sought friendship he'd never had
"Alone—bad"
The Bride disliked men and brothers
"She hate me like others"
The Monster looked at Pretorius and said, "We belong dead!"

Ygor's body was a wreck
"Frankenstein, they broke my neck"
"They wouldn't bury me in holy place like churchyard
Because I stole bodies—they said, so Ygor is dead!"
"Find Frankenstein's fiend!" the villagers cried
"The Monster had escaped and was ravaging the countryside"
The inspector stood bravely in his boots
"One doesn't easily forget Herr Baron, an arm torn out by the roots"

"Even a man who is pure in heart
And says his prayers by night
May become a wolf when the wolfbane blooms
And the autumn moon is bright"
"Evil spells, pentagram, wolfbane!
Oh, I'm sick of the whole thing
I'm going to get out of here!"
Larry Talbot; they couldn't understand
"Well, there's something very tragic about that man"
Larry's future was very grim
"Bela became a wolf and you killed him"
Talbot's torture would never end
"Tonight the moon will be full again!"

Dracula must hide where it is dark and dim
"Because a single ray of sunlight
Falling on a vampire will destroy him!"
Not all of the creatures lived on land
"It still doesn't prove the possibility of a gill man"
Abbott and Costello also discovered the monster lore
"Now that we've seen the last of Dracula,
The Wolf Man and the Monster
There's nobody to frighten us anymore"
There's a price to be paid by every horror fan
"Allow me to introduce myself, I'm the Invisible Man!"
"Quite a good scene, isn't it?
One man crazy, three very sane spectators"
"It reminds me of the broken battlements
Of my own castle in Transylvania"
"I am Count Dracula.
I am known to the outside world as Baron Latos."

1989

THE DEATH OF THE DARK DEMON

Gather 'round one and all
To hear a tale that be not small
It hath to do with one's desires
To fill the world with vampires

The legend comes from Europe of old
Around gypsy campfires it was told
Of the dark demon upon the hill
Whose death's purpose it was to kill

And when a kill was through and done
The victim would rise, but not in the sun
Nay, for only the light of the moon
Could strike this emissary of doom

This dark demon had eyes of red
To look upon them was to be dead
His lips were merely a cage
For his sharp white fangs of rage

The demon would fly out at night
Until a victim was in sight
Then he would withdraw his cloak
And sink his teeth into her throat

This went on for many a year
And brought to some more than a tear
Until one day a man brave and true
Knew quite well what he had to do

He found himself a sharp piece of wood
And hoped what he would do was good
He climbed that hill to the castle above
To seek vengeance for his lost love

He entered that place of awful sin
And found what was the demon's coffin
As he opened the lid his eyes could see
A monster more horrible there could never be

The sun was soon to be set
And the task was not done yet
Then the demon opened his eyes
And caught the man by total surprise

The demon grasped the man's mighty arm
To prevent it from doing the demon harm
But the man pushed them both through the open door
And onto the soft dirt of the misty moor

The man had to win no matter the cost
But the demon had downed him and all seemed lost
When suddenly in the darkness of the night
Came a floating form so bright

The form entered the man and gave him strength
To hold back the demon at short length
A cold sweat ran down his cheeks
His eyes bulged and he gritted his teeth

The demon's fangs drew closer to their mark
But the man had found the demon's heart
Though his hands were still to shake
That man drove in the wooden stake!

The demon let out a scream and then bowls of blood
To be mixed with the dirt and the mud
The man jumped up from this ground of gore
And stated of this, "He is no more!"

And of his kill knew this man
That it was his love that steadied his hand
And as he left this man could see
That his land would at last breathe free.

1976

THE FATE OF THE WEREWOLF

T'was a stormy night filled with fright
And horror happening soon
I was changed and my mouth was fanged
By the light of the first full moon

And as it continued to glow, fur began to grow
From my skin and I didn't know why
But I gave it thought as I strained and fought
And let out that terrible cry

My skin felt to burn as I rose to turn
To smash through the window and flee
Into to the night once more, this had happened before
To my forefathers, but not to me

The curse was old and often told
By the superstitious kind
They spoke of death and lost their breath
When corpses they would find

Of those mangled dead it was often said
Their veins were drained and dried
And before nightfall they would burn them all
No matter how hard they cried

My family had avoided the flames, but endured the pains
Of becoming a were-beast born
Though some would die by the silver cry
Few were there to mourn

I now knew the curse was mine as I gripped a STOP sign
Trying to control my rage
Who would believe or even conceive
A werewolf in this day and age?

I ran down the street in my new bare feet until I heard a sound
Though the wind blew the night, I saw the cigarette light
My victim had been found!

I carefully stalked him and his light would dim
As he heard my low tone growl
To his back I jumped, then slashed; I gnawed as well as gashed
And let out my victory howl
Being done with my feast I knew the beast was filled with glee
I had to give in order to live
The beast must remain quite free

Of civilization we could not bear
The noise as well as the air was not good
We left behind the metal and stones, the cars and the phones
For the "city" made of wood
The wind he blew and then we knew
Our running had brought us near
The forest stretched his arms to greet and we were soon to meet
The place we need not fear

But too much time had gone as we ran on
The sun began to rise
He did not leap, but fell to sleep and he closed our eyes
As myself again, I awoke, to find a man had spoke to me
"Why are you lying there?" he asked with a stare
And eyes that did not see

I told him my tale of woe and he asked me to go and follow him
He gave me a place to think with plenty of food and drink
But he wore the strangest grin
Of my beverage I was to sip, my mind began to slip
Into slumber once more
I laid upon the bed comforting my head and dreamed of before

Upon awakening I saw the stars through black metal bars
As well as the moon's powerful beam
I was trapped and caged and became quite enraged
As I let out his painful scream

The man owned a circus I found and would parade him around
In our little room
Though try as I might, there was no way to fight
The light of the second full moon.

1976

HAUNTED HALLOWEEN

Vampires, werewolves, ghouls and ghosts
Which does man fear the most?
Zombies and mummies; the living undead
Black cats and ravens with eyes of red
Witches fly broomsticks across the moon
Gremlins and goblins will be here soon
No one believes the things I've seen
Until they've had a Haunted Halloween

Folks are scared; can't you tell?
When Hunchback rings the tower bell
The bravest men are filled with fear
It only happens once a year
Halloween is finally here...

Christians call it the Devil's holiday
Refusing to allow their children to play
In costumes up and down the street
From door to door yelling, "Trick or Treat!"
Please let the little ones have their fun
It's not Satan worship on October thirty-one
No one believes the things we've seen
Until they've had a Haunted Halloween

They were pumpkins yesterday
Now Jack-o-lanterns light the way...

An ancient castle stands high on a hill
Upon its door hangs a funeral wreath
Death blows from its tower of shadows
Into its chamber of darkness underneath

Creatures on the loose – Monsters on the prowl
The Hangman's noose – A Wolf Man's howl
Nobody believes the things you've seen
Until they've had a Haunted Halloween!

1989

PERMANENT MARVELITE MAXIMUS

SURFER'S FATE

SUPER-HEROES

IRON DOOM

THE INCREDIBLE HULK

BRAND NEW

WHAT IF?

SURFER'S FATE

Zenn-La
Home of Norrin Radd
He who is the Silver Surfer

Galactus!
All-powerful cosmic being
Your sacrifice has made you his herald

Space
Upon your board
You search the cosmos for energy!

Shalla Bal
Her heart belongs to Norrin Radd
She waits an eternity for your return

Earth
Living beings
Your rebellion has made it your prison

Sky-rider of the spaceways
You are the Silver Surfer
And this is your fate.

1980

SUPER-HEROES

Captain America throws his shield
The Nazi Red Skull will never yield

Beneath the waves of the ocean dark
Swims the terrible Tiger Shark
Prince Namor is the ruler of the seas
The mighty Sub-Mariner, if you please

Loki schemes against brother Thor
While Fandral stands before Asgard's door

Hulk is on the rampage again
He'll soon square off with Abomination

Mephisto lurks in the depths of Hell
Doctor Strange relies on mystic spells

Spidey knows he mustn't fail
To avoid the whip of the Lizard's tail
Ducking Green Goblin's pumpkin barrage
Sidestepping Rhino's deadly charge
His spider-sense tingles when on alarm
That Doc Ock has unleashed his arms

The Mandarin concocts a master plan
To defeat invincible Iron Man

Ringmaster hypnotizes with his hat
But Daredevil's blindness took care of that

The Fantastic Four will always fight
The Frightful Four with all their might

The Masters of Evil are a bad bunch
The Avengers will match them punch for punch

The X-Men have entered the Danger Room
They all must face uncertain doom
When Super-heroes must defeat
Super-villains who are hard to beat!

Galactus tells Thing, "Earth's fate is sealed!"
So Sue casts forth her invisible field
Luckily Reed has Torch's fire
To bring back the Ultimate Nullifier

Colossus' strength and Cyclops' eye beam
Are powerfully teamed with Wolverine

The intangibility of the Vision
Forces Ultron to make a decision

The Falcon fights crime from on high
On his board, the Surfer rides the skies

Doctor Doom with cape unfurled
Devises ways to conquer the world!

Make Mine Marvel!

1985

IRON DOOM

Tony Stark, that's me; I'm weak at heart
Iron Man, I am so very smart
I will win each fight in which I shine my light
And they will feel my might 'cause I can't be hurt
(He can't be hurt)
I can't be hurt (He can't be hurt)

My idea of life is principle
My armor makes me invincible
Titanium, my foe with Crimson Dynamo
You give up; you know that I can't be hurt
"You can't be hurt"
I can't be hurt; "You can't be hurt"

Crime, I stop crime; that's always been my life story
I shouldn't mind 'cause I'm getting all the glory

Iron Man, that's me; I'm weak at heart
Tony Stark, I am so very smart
I've got cash and fame, even lots of dames
I'll win world acclaim 'cause I can't be hurt
(He can't be hurt)
I can't be hurt (He can't be hurt)

Crime, I stop crime; that's always been my life story
I shouldn't mind 'cause I'm getting all the glory

Doctor Doom is here, that evil jerk
Something's wrong, my suit, it doesn't work
Doctor Doom's blast ray is blowing me away
And I can hear him say, "Yes, you can be hurt!"
I can be hurt
"You can be hurt!"- I can be hurt...

Ooo—he zap me
Ooo—he zap me...

1979

THE INCREDIBLE HULK

He's the big man on your TV screen
He comes on Friday nights
Everybody says he's really mean 'cause all he does is fights

The incredible Hulk; the incredible Hulk
He's got a lot of bulk
So don't you sit and sulk
The incredible Hulk

He's really not all that bad when he makes the scene
But if you ever make him mad, he'll turn raging green

The incredible Hulk; the incredible Hulk
He's got a lot of bulk
So don't you sit and sulk
The incredible Hulk

He rips a new shirt nearly every day
And sometimes one at night
How his pants stay on; I just can't say
But they must be awfully tight

The incredible Hulk; the incredible Hulk
He's got a lot of bulk
So don't you sit and sulk
The incredible Hulk

Yes, Greenskin's just too big and strong
He smashes everything in sight
I would even doubt that old King Kong
Would mess with that mound of might!

The incredible Hulk; the incredible Hulk
He's got a lot of bulk
So don't you sit and sulk
The incredible Hulk.

1978

BRAND NEW

Brand new and waiting just for you
Ringing out the false and true
I'll show it to you now

Brand new
The condition is in mint
So pay another cent
Find that money somehow

Can you offer me a deal?
Pay for my next meal?
I'm a very desperate man
Can you understand the reason why
Collectors always seem to sigh?
I'm hoping that you can

I thought I would know it
But that's just not true
I'm going to blow it
I'll pass it on to you

Brand new
It just came out in June
Dealers play their greedy tune
They're ripping us off again

Brand new
X-Men never hit the stands
We'll never hold it in our hands
Unless we pay them off again

Thought I would know it
But that's just not true
I'm going to blow it
I'll pass it on to you
Brand new and waiting just for you...

1980

WHAT IF?

What if Spider-Man joined the Fantastic Four?
Would we really like them even more?
Would Jack have to draw those webs after all?
Or would Stan merely hang them back on the wall?

What if the Hulk had the brain of Bruce Banner?
Would Ross really react in a different manner?
Would Bruce not feel the bullets' sting?
Would we never see him fight the Thing?

What if the Avengers had never been?
Could Kang have been conquered by mortal men?
Would Captain America still be floating around?
Without the Avengers, he'd surely have drowned

What if the Invaders had stayed together after World War Two?
Could they have really made it through
The 40's and 50's without the real Cap?
Or would they have fallen into a trap?

And what if Captain America hadn't vanished during World War Two?
Would Bucky live on to wear his red, white and blue?
Could Cap really take Nick Fury's place
As director of SHIELD with an old face?

What if the Fantastic Four had different super-powers?
Would Reed never be able to hand Sue some flowers?
Would Johnny be the strong man and would Ben Grimm fly?
Could they destroy Doctor Doom on their first try?

What if the Watcher had never told us these tales?
Would Marvel see a slack in their sales?
I think not as we all can see
Marvel does it better, the best there can be.

1977

MOONDOG MANIA!

ROCK ALL NIGHT

OF PAUL

GO BULLDOGS!

DON'T LEAVE ME

LET'S GO

HE'S COMING FOR ME

THERE'S NO WAY TO BEAT INFLATION

THEY WANT SOME ICE CREAM!

PLAY IT BACK

SO LONG NOW

ROCK ALL NIGHT

Time for our show
Where is Ringo?
I don't know - ROCK!
We're gonna rock
ROCK ALL NIGHT!
Play drums for me
Where could he be?
I don't know - ROCK!
We're gonna rock
ROCK ALL NIGHT!

Great as X-Men both now and then
You love this band; give us a hand

We're in a trance
Give peace a chance
We're gonna rock—ROCK!
We're gonna rock
ROCK ALL NIGHT!
Paul plays guitar; George on sitar
Our name is: JOHN!
And of course, THE MOON DOGS!

San Francisco, we hate disco
But we still like "Goodnight Tonight"

Sing you a song; play all night long
We're gonna rock—ROCK!
We're gonna rock
ROCK ALL NIGHT!
We'll spin it on right up till dawn
We're gonna rock—ROCK!
We're gonna rock
ROCK ALL NIGHT!
Rock and roll all night...

1979

OF PAUL

While the Dreamer rests and lies around
The Birdman still sings at the speed of sound
Even back then it was his voice we heard
In only the best songs he sang every word

It was bound to happen; the end of the road
He went his own way to really explode
He was amazed; his love did it good
He let us in as only he could

We gave him the answer; he looked to the stars
We let him roll it to Venus and Mars
Charging like a ram with his band on the run
He makes his music to give us some fun

We called him back again in his own special way
To just see his face like it was yesterday
Like a titanium man, he gave us a show
It made us all feel like letting go

Told us love wasn't silly; got us hi, hi, hi
Taught us to say live and let die
We listened to what he said and he's not done yet
He's still flying high with wings on his jet.

1977

GO BULLDOGS!

Bulldogs—soaking up the sun
Bulldogs—having so much fun
We've got the spirit to win each and every fight
We can whip them anytime, be it day or night

Bat boy—grow into a man
That boy—what a super fan

We've got the power to beat them on our home field
They have yet to realize that we will never yield

You can score for me
You can score for me
You can score for me
If you're better, you can score for me!

Big fan—shouting in the stands
Nice plan—legendary hands
We've got the football and we never sing the blues
We still don't understand just what it is to lose

You can score for me
You can score for me
You can score for me
If you're better, you can score for me!

Go Bulldogs!
Go Bulldogs...

1979

DON'T LEAVE ME

Don't leave me, no, no, no!
Don't leave me, no, no, no!
Don't leave me, no, no, no, no

I said I wanted you but you said you had to go
And now I'm feeling blue, so please don't you hurt me so
I said, "Don't leave me"
I can't stand to be alone
Please don't leave me, you're the only girl I've known

I sent my heart to you
You sent me back a smile
You know I love you true
So won't you stay a while?

I said, "Don't leave me"
I can't stand to be alone
Please don't leave me, you're the only girl I've known

Don't leave me, no, no, no!
Don't leave me, no, no, no!
'Cause in my whole life, you're the only girl I've known

So what else can I say to make you stay with me?
I miss yesterday when we were both so free
I said, "Don't leave me"
I can't stand to be alone
Please don't leave me, you're the only girl I've known—you!

Don't leave me, no, no, no!
Don't leave me, no, no, no!
In my whole life, you're the only girl I've known
In my whole life, you're the only girl I've known
In my whole life, you're the only girl I've known

No, no, no! No, no, no, no.

1980

LET'S GO

I'm leaving town, won't you come with me?
Blue eyes brown crying into the sea

Let's go (let's get it on)
Let's go (then we'll be gone)
Let's go (let's get it on)
Pack up your bags 'cause I said "Let's go"
(Pack up your bags) 'cause I said "Let's go"

I loved you and you tore me apart
So untrue that you broke my heart

Let's go (let's get it on)
Let's go (then we'll be gone)
Let's go (let's get it on)
Pack up your bags 'cause I said "Let's go"
(Pack up your bags) 'cause I said "Let's go"

You're holding back 'cause there's another man
You tell Mac that you've changed your plans

Let's go (let's get it on)
Let's go (we will be gone)
Let's go (let's get it on)
Pack up your bags 'cause I said "Let's go"
(Pack up your bags) 'cause I said "Let's go!"

Oh baby, let's go
(Let's get it on)
Then outside we'll go
(Let's get it on)
Let's go
Oh baby, let's go, go, go, go, go!
I said "Let's go!"
Oh yeah, let's go
Let's go, go, go, go, go, go....

1980

HE'S COMING FOR ME

He's coming for me
What will I do?
He's gonna floor me -I'm black and blue
I'm always running from her boyfriend
He's coming for me
Looks like the end!

His fists are hurting
He beats me up
'Cause I was flirting with his buttercup
I can't stop running
I'll never mend
He's coming for me
Looks like the end!

Fight, I don't fight over the girl I love
I believe my strength lies within my heart not in my glove

Yet I still like her
Am I insane?
And here comes Mike, sir
Oh what a pain!
I must do something to make her mine
He's coming for me
I'm out of time!

Fight, I don't fight over the girl I love
I believe my strength lies within my heart not in my glove

He's coming for me
What can I do?
He's gonna floor me - I'm black and blue
I'm always running from her boyfriend
He's coming for me
Looks like the end!

1979

THERE'S NO WAY TO BEAT INFLATION

There's no way to beat inflation
Go and spend all your money right now
Everyone across the nation
Is feeling the pinch somehow

Hey Iran, you have the oil
That I need to drive my car
If you don't send us the oil
Then I can't drive very far

Today I drove to Exxon
To buy all I could get
I paid a dollar per gallon
To pump my gas, premium
Of course for my Corvette

There's no way to beat inflation
Go and spend all your money right now
Everyone across the nation
Is feeling the pinch somehow

The U.S. has its great dollar
And it ain't worth one thin dime
So why not raise your prices?
Then you will be doing fine

Your new plan still has one problem
Your friends will raise prices too
So you mark up your items
Inflation, yes it's true

There's no way to beat inflation
Go and spend all your money right now
Everyone across the nation
Is feeling the pinch somehow.

1979

THEY WANT SOME ICE CREAM!

Here they come as we all run to have some fun and they all fall forever
Trip down the stairs and leave all your cares
Just leave it all
They're falling...

Wiping off the counter
Wiping off the dust and stains
Almond toffee ice cream, leaving early Monday
Yawn, it's been a boring day
I just thought up this song

They want some yogurt
They want some sherbert
They want some ice cream!
Cha-cha-cha-chocolate!

Frozen pineapple sherbert cracking apart like pineapple in the sun
It tastes so sweet like sugar with a beat
Trip down the stairs
They're falling...
They're falling...

Red raspberry yogurt drooling from a fat girl's mouth
Homogenized whole milk
Yicky-sticky yogurt
Man, that is an awful taste there in those eight ounce cups

They want some yogurt
They want some sherbert
They want some ice cream!
Va-va-vanilla!

Running through the Dairy Science building down the hall
If you don't run you get a man who's falling down the dairy steps
They're falling...
They're falling...
They're falling...

They want some yogurt
They want some sherbert
They want some ice cream!

Extra texture lemon custard
Can't you find the mustard in the fridge?
Trip down the stairs
Forget all your cares
Just leave it all

They're falling...
They're falling...
They're falling...
They're falling...

Strawberry yogurt spilling in the pineapple punch
Tropical chocolate, cherry and vanilla
Gross, they could have been eating the dry cottage cheese

They want some yogurt
They want some sherbert
They want some ice cream!

1980

PLAY IT BACK

I'll tell you now!
(I'm going to explain everything)
You'll know it all!
Walrus was Paul, oh yeah...

I love you, my diamond girl
Dreamer rests
He gave you a life
I'll take you for my wife

Birdman has wings
Birdman has wings
Birdman has wings
Birdman has wings
Fly...

Here comes our bat boy
I think that his name is Roy
And there is our big fan
He's shouting all over the stands

X-Men search for Doctor Doom
But he's not in either room
They have asked Titanium Man
He doesn't seem to understand

Crimson Dynamo won't tell them
Exactly where Doom has been
They will try to force his hand
Avenge the death of Iron Man

Doctor Doom has slipped away again...

I'm not done yet!
(We've still got a little ways to go)
Listen to me
Then you will see the light...

I tried to get away from him
But my future looked very grim
You know I don't know how to fight
So why don't we call it a night?
Everything will be all right

You know that I'll always like her
Please leave us alone Mike, sir
So he hit me right in the face
I believe that I lost my place
It's such a big disgrace

Cindy loved Michael and they had planned to be wed
Michael had been a werewolf man
She shot him
Now both he and their love are dead

Werewolf Man
Werewolf Man
You're cursed by the full moon

Werewolf Man
Werewolf Man
The only cure is doom

I told you so!
(Play it back again)
Now that you know
It's time to go right now…

Play it back if you ever have a chance to hear it all again
Play it back if you ever have a chance to hear it all again
Play it back if you ever have a chance to hear it all again
Play it back if you ever have a chance to hear it all again
Play it back if you ever have a chance to hear it all again
Play it back if you ever have a chance to hear it all again
Play it back if you ever have a chance to hear it all again.

1980

SO LONG NOW

This is finally our last album
Yes it is, but don't feel bad
A reception or perception
Of our group has made me glad

I have never been more happy
With singers and songs that I sang with you
Most were grand and few were boring
So long now, I'll miss you too

'Cause without these songs and singers
My life will be simple once more
And I'll listen to the ladies
And I'll dream of things the night before

You know I always will remember
Paul McGear and times we had such fun
I know you'll never sing and shout anymore
So long now, your time has come

You know I always will remember
Paul McGear and times we had back then
I know you'll never sing and shout anymore
So long now, it is the end
So long now, it is the end.

1979

ANOTHER WAY

ANOTHER WAY

Here we sit with candles lit and music in our ears
Wine in hand and Pepper's Band hides us from our fears

But we know if we don't go death will claim us soon
Drifting in then through our skin
Play his haunting tune

Say, we'd better find another way
Say, before we lose another day

Tears of rain cause so much pain for young men who must sign
To fight a war they don't care for to keep the oil pipeline

Say, we've got to find another way
Say, before we lose another day

Deep in space lives another race unlike you and me
If we can we'll take their hands
Make it differently

Why can't we, just you and me
Please let me hear you say,
"Let's make love in the stars above
We'll find another way"

Say, we'd better find another way
Say, now just where does our future lay?

1980

BET

Bet...Bet...Bet!

You can always gamble away your good money
Because you know that I know that it has never stopped you before
So bet...
You have your funny money to make even more!

Bet...Bet...Bet!

You have always thought of going to Las Vegas
Why did you take out that big loan before the price was set?
So bet...you are so wealthy with your money
Buy a Corvette!
Bet!

Your money, won't bet to always have it
Your money, won't bet to always have it
Your money...so funny

So bet...
You are so wealthy with your money
Buy a Corvette!

Bet!
You can always gamble away your good money
Why don't you just go for broke now and give it a shot?
So bet...you are so wealthy with your money
Buy a Corvette!

So bet...
You are so wealthy with your funny money
Buy a Corvette!

Your funny money
Your funny money...yes.

1980

144

BEAUTIFUL LOVE

Give me all your time so I'll finally see
Beautiful love
Something above
And something for you and me
Beautiful love together

Hearing you talking through my phone
I'm comprehending what you say
I'm feeling good about myself and now it comes through
I have to find another way

Give me all your time so I'll finally see
Beautiful love
Something above
And something for you and me
Beautiful love together

Someone you know has seen me there
She gets her things and then she goes
But then I can't, I show no one and she's gone away
And that's what really makes me sad

Give me all your time so I'll finally see
Beautiful love
Something above
And something for you and me
Beautiful love together
Beautiful love together
Beautiful love together.

1980

LAND OF THE SUN

Trapped within my own mind
Tucked away forever
Never singing love songs any more
Help me, lady…me…lady…me…

I've got to wake myself up
I've got to show the whole world
I'm not dreaming my life away
Just give me a date with you, girl
I've got to wake myself up
(You've got to wake yourself up)

Then the light came on complete with golden rays
So I began to run
And my left eye looked while my other eye looked
They saw it all undone

Land of the sun, land of the sun
With the velvet sky that was so high
It's straight to number one in the land of the sun…

Well, now my life has changed in so many ways
It could happen to anyone
'Cause it's the greatest place that I've ever known
To see the secrets of the sun!

Land of the sun, land of the sun
With the velvet sky that was so high
It's straight to number one in the land of the sun…

Now my girl is calling to show me something about the land of sun
We will love each other and live forever and we want you all to come!

Land of the sun, land of the sun
With the velvet sky that was so high
It's straight to number one in the land of the sun…

1980

146

WHISPERS

In the cave of the quiet ones
We have heard
It is said
Those who live there are dead

They wear their black robes
And we never see their faces
But we know their movements leave traces

Shhh...silent we must be
And only speak in whispers
If they were to hear you
You might not see tomorrow
So please, only speak in whispers.

1980

NO SAY NO

Now we're just cruisin' all over town
We can't drive slower
We can't look down
We can't even let you know, but we can go...

No...say no, No...say no
No...say no, No...say no

You have heard "That Kinda Man"
You understand the Panda Man
Don't talk to the Panda Man

Our next song is "Death Rock Row"
You better go, you Panda Man
Don't talk to the Panda Man

We don't believe you're a relative
We've got trouble tonight so look out...
Don't talk to the Panda Man
Don't talk to the Panda Man
Don't talk to the Panda Man

No...say no, No...say no
No...say no, No...say no

You said you like "Texas Death"
Don't hold your breath for "10 Degrees"
By the way, we don't agree

Don't talk to the Panda Man
Don't talk to the Panda Man
Don't talk to the Panda Man

We don't believe you're a relative
We've got trouble tonight so look out...
No...say no, No...say no...

1980

148

DOCTOR HOLLYRIDGE

In the songs the Moondogs sang
There was muzak to be played
And it was so very bad
In the strings of Hollyridge

So we used all that we could
Kept it cold inside the fridge
And we sang all of those songs
By the doctor, Hollyridge

How I hate you, Doctor Hollyridge
Doctor Hollyridge, Doctor Hollyridge

But we still used all your songs
O'Boogie thought of them as all wrong
And I still despise them now...

How I hate you, Doctor Hollyridge
Doctor Hollyridge, Doctor Hollyridge

Now we know he is a creep
'Cause he puts us all to sleep
The doctor's office plays his tunes
You'd better move away to Saturn's moons

Now I got so very high
I'm sure you know, I touched the sky
I have walked over that bridge
Built by Doctor Hollyridge

How I hate you, Doctor Hollyridge
Doctor Hollyridge, Doctor Hollyridge

How I hate you, Doctor Hollyridge
Doctor Hollyridge, Doctor Hollyridge...

1980

BE MY LOVER

Call me up when I'm all alone
I need someone to talk to
'Cause your voice will always do

Be my lover, be my lover
Be my lover
Yeah, yeah, yeah

Hold my hand when I need you to
It's my broken heart again
Only you can help it mend

Be my lover, be my lover
Be my lover
Yeah, yeah, yeah
Lover, ah-ha
Lover, ah-ha

Don't be cold 'cause I'm hot for you
And I think you know it now
That I'll get to you somehow

Be my lover, be my lover
Be my lover
Yeah, yeah, yeah
Lover, ah-ha
Lover, ah-ha

Kiss me now and let me lean on you
Girl, I really need you so
And I'll never let you go

Be my lover, be my lover
Be my lover
Yeah, yeah, yeah...

1980

THINK OF ME

The rich young gambler lost his bet
His winnings on the wheel
But though he lost he took it well
And made himself a new deal

Think of me
Think of my wealth
I know that I've seen better days
Think of me
Think of my wealth
I know that I've seen better days

It was late in the evening
I was a feeling so bad
Then I saw you were leaving
Please don't go away from me, darling
Please don't go and make me sad

Please think of me
Think of my wealth
I know that I've seen better days
Think of me
Think of my wealth
I know that I've seen better days

Bet...Bet
Bet...Bet

Think of me
Think of my wealth
I know that I've seen better days
Think of me - Think of my wealth
I know I have seen better days

No...say no, No...say no
No...say no, No...say no...

1980

DEATH CAN TAKE YOU

Death has claimed you my one-time friend
You will be missed
Oh no...come back to me

Goodbye to those who died
Forever young
We will miss you so much now
Please come back to us again somehow
What will we do to show that we still need you?

Oh yeah, I'll play you again
Death will never let you go and it hurts us so

Death can take you
Death can take you
Death can take you any time

You'd better beware of the Reaper
You'd better beware of the Reaper
You'd better beware of the Reaper
The Grim Reaper
The Grim Reaper
The Grim Reaper!

Now you have passed away and we'll never forget this day
You meant so much to all of us, it's true
So we have come to say so long and we hope we can be as strong
Pretty soon we're all gonna be dead too

Death...Death

Death can take you.

1980

ANOTHER WAY (REPRISE)

All the cheers have turned to tears
On this most tragic day
End of life witnessed by his wife
John Lennon has passed away

We loved John but now he's gone
He died a Sixties death
Anything that he would sing
We listened to every breath

Say, we lost the Dreamer yesterday
Say, now he has found another way

Yes he's gone, but his dream lives on
In the music that he made
He gave us much to discuss
He finally made the grade

It's so sad 'cause he's all we had
Told us what must be done
To enhance, give peace a chance
The world will live as one

Say, he didn't believe in yesterday
Say, we've got to find another way

Say, we'd better find another way
Say, before we lose another day

(John is dead. Miss him, miss him).

December 9, 1980

MAYBE

Yeah! Yeah! Yeah!
Let's sing more songs...

They were the greatest band the world has ever known
Let's see what we can do now that we have grown
We must still take the time before we take the world
Let's see what we can do...

They had it planned so well
They were number one
Let's see what we can do
We've had our dry run

We must still take the time before we take the world
Let's see what we can do...

Give me a chance to learn how to play a bass
If we are good enough, we can find a space

Oh...maybe we can
Wo, wo, wo—maybe so

Maybe we can
Form a new band

Oh...maybe we can
Wo, wo, wo—maybe so

Oh, we've got ladders to climb
Taking our time
We've got ladders to climb

What's in store in '84?

Oh...maybe we can...

1980

UP THESE LADDERS OF LIFE

LONG LONELY CLIMB
I CAN'T SEE YOU
THE BUTTERFLY AND THE CHAMELEON
NEVER CAME BACK
ROCKSTAR
GIRLS ARE SO DIFFERENT
HERE WE ARE
MY BABY AND I
MR. ROMANCE AND THE SWINGING KID
GOING BACK
THE SEARCH
THE CORNER CONCEPT
POCKETS OF TIME
THIS OLD HOUSE
NOBODY LIKE ME

LONG LONELY CLIMB

It's been a long lonely climb
It's been a long, long lonely climb
It's been a long...lonely...climb...
It's been a long lonely climb up these ladders of life
I'll never reach the top but I can never stop this long, long lonely climb
Every step of the way has been a struggle
Every step of the way has been hard
But with each one I do, it brings me closer to you
And that's why I can't disregard
This long lonely climb
It's been a long, long lonely climb
It's been a long...lonely...climb...

It's been a long lonely climb up these ladders of life
I'll never reach the top but I can never stop this long, long lonely climb
Climbing up has taken all of my efforts
Climbing up has taken all of my time
But I make no mistake with each step I take
On this long, long lonely climb
It's been a long lonely climb
It's been a long, long lonely climb
It's been a long...lonely...climb...
Step after step, I'm climbing into the clouds
Right after left, I'm making my way
But you know that it's true that I really love you
And I'm trying to make it better today!

Every step of the way has been a struggle
Climbing up has taken all of my time
But with each one I do, it brings me closer to you
And I make no mistake with each step I take
But you know that it's true that I really love you
And I'm trying to make it better today!
It's been a long lonely climb
It's been a long, long lonely climb
It's been a long...lonely...climb.

1981

I CAN'T SEE YOU

I can't see you - no, no, no-no, no, no, no
I can't see you - I can't see you
Why I can't see you

I have been to your house
Why, I've even seen your face
But it was just a photograph
That was taken out of place

I have written all my current dreams
Now my pen is running dry
I have mailed you all the hearts I have
All I want is your reply

I can't see you- no, no, no-no, no, no, no
I can't see you - I can't see you
Why I can't see you

If you show yourself to me
Then I'll show you what I do
If you give yourself to me
Then I'll give myself to you

Reflections of the past are cast upon the lake
Where moonlight mends our minds till morning we shall wake
To see the sun that shines upon the love we make

I can't see you – you won't see me
I still want you in my dream to be
I call you up on the phone
But words are all we say
I have been so all alone
Won't you come with me to stay?

I can't see you
I can't see you, babe.

1981

THE BUTTERFLY AND THE CHAMELEON

I'm just a butterfly blowing in the breeze
I'm just a butterfly flying past the trees
Though I'm a butterfly, I think of different things
Even a butterfly must spread his colored wings

You're the chameleon, you change your colors well
Hiding certain secrets that you will never tell
You're a chameleon making every move
You're the chameleon with nothing left to prove

But if you knew what you do to me
Maybe it would make you see
If you knew what you do to me

When I'm watching you my heart lets out a sigh
I want so much to touch you
Instead I only cry
Though you drive me crazy with the changes you go through
That will never stop me from always loving you

Yes, I am the butterfly blowing in the breeze
I'm just a butterfly, won't you help me please?
You're the chameleon, you've shown that you are strong
Sometimes I can see you and sometimes I am wrong

When we've come together it's always been as friends
Is it nothing more than that or is it just pretend?

The butterfly and the chameleon
There is nothing more to say
Either give your heart to me
Or watch me fly away

But if you knew what you do to me
Maybe it would make you see
If you knew what you do to me.

1981

NEVER CAME BACK

So we jumped out on 285
What would they say if we didn't arrive?
Can't slow down; keep up with the pack
What would they say if we never came back?

We've always been fast
They know that's true
What have they got against me and you?
We've been drilled to the floor and nailed to the wall
Just give us a chance and we'll make the call

We all must understand why we are the way we are
People change but they stay the same
Drivers switch from car to car

I can't decide what I want to do most of all
Too many things and too many dreams keeping me on the ball

Faster and faster the world spins around
Spinning my life away
I want to be with you but there's too much to do
And it's not getting done today

Your foot's to the floor, but the ride has been rough
What if we said, "It's time to get tough!"
Put away the past with all of its "ping"
Now we're high strung and ready to sting!

Never, never come back
Never, never come back
Far away from me
Far away from me

Never, never come back
Never, never come back
Keep it cool and free
Loveless odyssey

We've gotta keep going
Can't run out of gas
What would they say if we didn't last?
You better brace yourselves for another attack
What would they say if we never came back?

Life is white
Go make your mark
Into the light
Stay out of the dark

Your life is white
Gotta add some black
Put black on white
And never look back

A love comes along that takes you aside
They have to be strong
Our faith hasn't died
If luster we lack then you'd better believe
If we never came back then we never should leave

So we jumped out on 285
What would they say if we didn't arrive?
Can't slow down; keep up with the pack
What would they say if we never came back?

Perimeter... Pascual Perez...
Perimeter... Pascual Perez...
Perimeter... Pascual Perez...

1983

ROCKSTAR

In the lives of young men who try hard now and then
To make a kind of music with just a bit of sin
The lights are dancing so bright that the crowd is out of sight
But the band just keeps on playing on into the night

Rockstar
Tell me who you are and where you think you're going to
Rockstar
Just be what you are and take all the things we're showing you

They may not play so very good or sound just like they should
They may be just a little bit off, but they're so misunderstood
The beat goes on, they try so well and only time will tell
For will their music make it?
Will those lyrics sell?

Rockstar
In your fancy car driving up the avenue
Rockstar
If you drive very far you might find there is something new

Rockstar
Tell me who you are and where you think you're going to
Rockstar
Just be what you are and take all the things we're showing you
Rockstar
If you drive too far you may find other Rockstars just like you!

1982

GIRLS ARE SO DIFFERENT

Girls are so different in so many ways
Girls are so different, what can I say?
They take hold of your heart and then walk away
Girls can be different as night is from day

Girls are expensive; they spend all of your pay
They still ask for more, I have to say, "Nay"
Girls are so different, ooo but I say,

I can't get enough of 'em – I really do love 'em
Love 'em, love 'em, love 'em, love 'em, love 'em to death
Love 'em, love 'em, love 'em, love 'em, love 'em to death
And I keep up my guard 'cause they squeeze me so hard
That I can't......catch my breath

But she's not the one your heart beats for
She's not the one knocking on your door
She's not the one who lives above
And she's not the one you want to love

Girls are so different in so many ways
Girls are so different, what can I say?
They take hold of your heart and then walk away
Girls can be different as night is from day

I can't get enough of 'em - I really do love 'em
Love 'em, love 'em, love 'em, love 'em, love 'em to death
Love 'em, love 'em, love 'em, love 'em, love 'em to death
And I keep up my guard 'cause they squeeze me so hard
That I can't......catch my breath

I think I'm in love, what can I say?
Girls are so different - Please keep it that way

Girls are so different...
They certainly are...different.

1983

HERE WE ARE

Here we are
Here we are
Here we are
Just wishing on a star
Not getting very far
Here we are

Where are they?
Where are they?
Where are they?
Not living for today
They want to go away
Where are they?

To my friend
To my friend
To my friend these hands I'll lend
This love I send to my friend

Need you too
Need you too
Need you too
Don't know what I'd do if I didn't have you
Need you too

Love you so
Love you so
Love you so
Thought I'd let you know that I love you so
Love you so

Here we are living on this Earth for what our lives are worth
That means everything goes on
We'll try to make you see it doesn't have to be
'Cause everything goes on
Everything grows on

Remember John
Remember John
Remember John
His dream lives on
We gotta carry on
Remember John

Gotta hope
Gotta hope
Gotta hope
Don't hang by a rope
Don't slip on the soap
Gotta hope

Live in peace
Live in peace
Live in peace
Let the fighting cease
Don't sign a lease
Live in peace

Don't you cry
Don't you cry
Don't you cry
Don't ever say goodbye
We're never gonna die
Don't you cry

Here we are
Here we are
Here we are
Just wishing for a star
Not getting very far
Here we are

Here we are!

1983

MY BABY AND I

My baby and I went out last night
We missed the curfew, but that's all right
My baby and I know how to rock
We rolled all over till three o'clock

But my baby and I stayed out too late
Trying to make the most of every date
When we got home, her door was locked
My baby and I had over-rocked
Rock on...

Went around back where she snuck in
Nobody knew she wasn't home by 10:00
So my baby and I are doing all right
Maybe next time, we'll rock all night!

1983

MR. ROMANCE AND THE SWINGING KID

Mr. Romance goes home at night to watch his baseball game
The Swinging Kid is out of sight like a man who's lost his name
Romance knows nobody else to share his little world
The Kid must look inside himself; they both must find a girl

For half a decade they have known each other through thick and thin
Time has passed as they have grown to long like normal men
They long to have a stable life; to finally settle down
They long to have a loving wife—ain't no fooling around

Mr. Excitement is a bore; everything is set for him
Though his friends have fun in store he turns his back on them
Mr. Reliable might be there, the Kid can never tell
Nobody said that life is fair; Romance knows this all too well

Mr. Romance and the Swinging Kid
Their loves seem to come and go
It's time for them to pop the lid and find what they already know
Mr. Romance and the Swinging Kid say it's worse to rent than to own
Could it be something that they did?
Perhaps that's why they live alone

Mr. Danger has gone away careful as he could be
Maybe they'll meet again someday then there will be three
Three who have a major goal to make all fighting cease
Love and music will make them whole and give them inner peace

For half a decade they have known each other through thick and thin
Time has passed as they have grown to long like normal men

Mr. Romance and the Swinging Kid
Their loves seem to come and go
It's time for them to pop the lid and find what they already know
Mr. Romance and the Swinging Kid say it's worse to rent than to own
Could it be something that they did?
Perhaps that's why they sleep alone.

1984

GOING BACK

Going back to China Town
Going to sit my baby down
We're gonna do some talking tonight
Going back to get my girl
Going to show her all the world
I'm gonna make it work out right

Going back where I belong
Going to learn to get along
Going to put an end to the fight
Going back to China Town
Going to sit my baby down
We're gonna do some talking tonight

These are the times of our lives
The very best times of our lives
Please don't let them go - No...No!

Going back to London Town
Going to take a look around
Going to make some music today
Going back to find my band
Going to hope they understand
Gonna make them get up and play

Going back where I belong
Going to learn to sing along
Never going to throw it away
Going back to London Town
Going to play some gigs around
Gonna do some rocking today

These are the times of our lives
The very best times of our lives
Please don't let them go - No...No!

1985

THE SEARCH

I'm so restless; can't get to sleep
Tossing and turning under the sheet
Body ablaze; mind's on fire
Got to search now before I lose the desire

Cancel the bars; not into that scene
Got my car, an attractive machine
I'll get dates, but the girls are all wrong
I can't wait until the end of this song

The search is on for the girl of my dreams
The search goes on; she is not what she seems
The search goes on; can't afford to relax
The search goes on...gotta face the facts...

The search for the one who will always be true
It hasn't been easy, but I'll continue
The search goes on
How long will it take?
The search goes on until it's too late...

Looking ahead, I'll spot her on sight
Then I'll ask her, "Is this finally right?"
Don't want one too young
Don't want one too old
Avoid the extremes; that's what I've been told

There's always the doubt she'll never be found
My luck runs out if she was never around
The search will go on
I'll look high and low
Will I be married or remain a solo?

1985

THE CORNER CONCEPT

We're in our corners and I say that's fine
We share the same room, but this half is mine
Stay on your side, that's where you belong
"Mind your own business"
That's the point of this song

Everybody's doing their own thing
All caught up in their little world, hey!
People, you don't know what you're missin'
C'mon, take the time to listen
Stand up and leave your corner behind
Take a walk toward the other side, yeah!
Shake the hand of a total stranger
He won't bite, so what's the danger?

I'll put up a barrier so he can't get through
I keep to myself and you'd better too
I've got my own interests so leave me alone
Don't want your friendship
Don't call on the phone!

I see someone seeking the sunshine
They wanted to make the first move
Open up, let's come together
Have some fun; enjoy the weather
Too many people are fading away
Crawling into caves and corners
Get up and take a walk outside
Don't keep looking for a place to hide

I've got to decide between the things that you've said
And the things that I'm doing that are stuck in my head
So I might come out 'cause maybe I'm wrong
If you say that you'll help me, I'll try to belong
I'll try to belong, I'll try to belong
Yes, I will, I'll try to belong...

1987

POCKETS OF TIME

You gotta keep looking for those pockets of time
You gotta keep looking for those pockets of time
You gotta keep looking for those pockets of time
You know you've got a lot of things to do
And your screaming schedule is getting to you
You gotta keep looking for those pockets of time

You drove up and down, all over Cross Town
Trying to track that certain item down
Only to find that it couldn't be found
You gotta keep looking for those pockets of time

You gotta keep looking for those pockets of time
You gotta keep looking for those pockets of time
You gotta keep looking for those pockets of time
Errands to run, but there's places to be
Things not getting done, but you'll learn to see
You gotta keep looking for those pockets of time

You go to the bank and you go to the store
The clocks keep ticking for you to do more
The pressure is building like never before
You gotta keep looking for those pockets of time

You gotta keep looking for those pockets of time
Counting clues at the scene of the crime
You gotta keep looking for those pockets of time
Calls to make and appointments to keep
A job to work and no time to sleep!
You gotta keep looking for those pockets of time

A structured schedule is all that you've seen
And some of those meetings can be mighty mean
So take advantage of the times in between

You gotta keep looking for those pockets of time.

1988

THIS OLD HOUSE

Long ago before the great war
My grandfather lived in his store
Because he had no place of his own
He married and a house was bought
They settled in and then they thought
"This old house will always be our home"

Children were born and one was my Dad
They played in these rooms, what fun they had
Living in the best place they had known
They soon grew up and moved away
Only my Dad remained to say,
"This old house will always be my home"

This old house has stood the test of many generations
Though very modest, it's still the best for me and my relations

Dad married Mom and they did the chores
Cleaning the windows and mopping the floors
But the spaciousness made them feel all alone
So I was born right under this roof
And as I grew, I needed no proof
That this old house would always be my home

This old house has stood the test of many generations
Though very modest, it's still the best for me and my relations

Still living here with my wife
And a son added to our life
Loving him always till he's grown
He talks of this place wherever he goes
Deep in his heart I think he knows
This old house will always be his home

This old house has stood the test of many generations
Though very modest, it's still the best for me and my relations.

1988

NOBODY LIKE ME

Watch the people when you go out
And tell me what you think
One does this and one does that
You wonder, "What's the link?"

But the truth is they're all unique
And that's what makes the world go 'round
And there's nobody like you
And nobody can be
And there's no one, nobody like me

God created everyone that lives upon this Earth
And no two people can be alike from the moment of their birth
Everyone is different and that's what makes the world go 'round
And there's nobody like you
And nobody can be
And there's no one, nobody like me

Billions and billions have been here before
Billions and billions will come after I'm gone
Billions and billions of personalities on and on and on...

It's astonishing to realize that these thoughts are my own
No one else can share these dreams
They're mine and mine alone
Imagining a new idea is what makes the world go 'round
And there's nobody like you
And nobody can be
And there's no one, nobody like me

Please don't you hang your head and feel worthless on this day
You're as special as I am and that's why I always say
Everyone contributes something to make this world go 'round
And there's nobody like you
And nobody can be
And there's no one, nobody like me.

1989

AFTERWORD

So that's it for now. I hope if you made it this far that you have been entertained along the way. I never set out to be a great poet in the likes of Robert Frost, Emily Dickinson or Edgar Allan Poe. My goal was simply to write things that came to me or could somehow fit the project we were working on at the time. Some attempts were more successful than others and you have them now to read and re-read as often as you'd like. If anything, perhaps they can serve as a distraction for whenever you might need one.

Please feel free to pass this book on to others. Particularly young people—teenagers, to be exact. You see, if you're going to be a poet, or a writer of any sort, I believe that's where it begins. I wrote my first real poem when I was sixteen. For the next fourteen years, they just kept coming in one way or another. I couldn't stop them, so I embraced them. Then suddenly, when I was on the verge of thirty years old—they stopped. I cannot explain it, but it does not seem uncommon for those extra creative, inspirational juices to dry up when we begin our fourth decade of life.

It is a fact that every song written and recorded by the Beatles was done so before any of them had reached thirty years in age. Now they each went on to have successful solo careers in their thirties, but no one would argue that they ever equaled what they accomplished while in their twenties. At one time, the working title for this book was "The Teens and Twenties" because I firmly believe these are the most fertile years for creativity of any kind.

I strongly encourage those in this age bracket to make the most of your inspirations during this time. For me, it was poetry writing and recording. For you, it might be engineering, cinematography, inventions or music composition. Work at it with a sense of urgency as it may well be the greatest accomplishment of your entire life.

The more quality output you create while in your twenties, the stronger your base and background will be for later on in life. Hopefully, you can still continue to create quality works in whatever field you are in for decades to come. Just don't miss the window while you are young.

As for me, now in my fiftieth year of life, I hope my work on compiling this volume will inspire me to pick up the craft again. I can tell for that to happen, it will have to be much more forced than before. Gone are the nights when the lyrics just appeared in my head. Gone are the days when a whole poem could be completed from just a working title on a paper.

However, my hope is that by making a conscious effort to write and rhyme, a new creative inspiration will strike me. New ideas will flow and new directions can be explored. Perhaps I will not be able to come up with anything to equal the best pieces included in this book. I've set my own standard and it's up to me to take that as a challenge. I can only try my best and be grateful for whatever the Lord gives me.

Thank you for reading.

C. Cooper Ard

Contact: clintard@email.com

THANK YOU LORD JESUS

Thank you Lord Jesus
For saving my life
Thank you Lord Jesus
For my loving wife

Thank you Lord Jesus
For my daughter and son
Thank you sweet Jesus
For all that you've done

You're my sun
You're my moon
You're my day and my night
You're everything good
You're everything right

You're my wisdom
You're my strength
You're the grain in my field
You're my spirit
You're my soul
You're my sword and my shield

Thank you Lord Jesus
For my happy home
Thank you Lord Jesus
That I'm not alone

Thank you Lord Jesus
For family and friends
Thank you sweet Jesus
Your love never ends

Amen.

178

INDEX OF TITLES

Titles of lyrics are followed by the title of the audio or printed collection where the work first appeared.

a minor matter = *audio EP cassette, the Ladders*
Automatic Overdrive = *audio album cassette, the Ladders*
Baxter Street = *audio album cassette, the Moondogs*
Black on White = *audio album cassette, the Ladders*
Climbing Thru the Eighties = *audio album cassette, the Ladders*
Coup = *1978 magazine, Minot State College*
Different Panes of Glass = *audio album cassette, the Ladders*
First Step = *audio album cassette, the Ladders*
Gear Fab Band = *audio album cassette, the Moondogs*
Home is the Hero = *poetry collection, C. Cooper*
Image = *1976–1977 magazine, Bellevue High School*
Let Us Live = *audio album cassette, the Moondogs*
Out of This World = *audio album cassette, the Moondogs*
Recollections = *audio album cassette, the Ladders*
Rock All Night = *audio album cassette, the Moondogs*
Separate Roads = *poetry collection, C. Cooper*
The Baggers = *audio album cassette, the Baggers*
Through the Eyes of One = *poetry collection, C. Cooper*
Triple Versions = *audio album cassette, John O'Boogie*

www.ingramcontent.com/pod-product-compliance
Lightning Source LLC
Chambersburg PA
CBHW022022090426
42739CB00006BA/247